Grandparenting

with the

Wisdom of Nature

Empower your grandchild for life
with 7 simple principles

Barbara Joyce Frank, Ph.D.

First Printing, 2012

Printed in the United States of America

Liability Disclaimer

By reading this book, you assume all risks associated with using the advice given below, with a full understanding that you, solely, are responsible for anything that may occur as a result of putting this information into action in any way, and regardless of your interpretation of the advice.

You further agree that our company cannot be held responsible in any way for the success or failure of your business as a result of the information presented in this book. It is your responsibility to conduct your own due diligence regarding the safe and successful operation of your business if you intend to apply any of our information in any way to your business operations.

Terms of Use

You are given a non-transferable, "personal use" license to this book. You cannot distribute it or share it with other individuals.

Also, there are no resale rights or private label rights granted when purchasing this book. In other words, it's for your own personal use only.

Table Of Contents

Introduction

The book you hold in your hand is a call to action. It is a rallying cry, urging you away from society's stagnant stereotypes of grandparenthood and back into the vibrant cycle of life. Nature is out there, waiting for you and your grandchild to return to it hand-in-hand. It is waiting to give you its gifts of wisdom and healing. As you step *into* this book, please also step *outward*, into a wider and *wilder* world that takes "Grandma" and "Grandpa" into the truly "grand" realms of Mother Earth and Father Sky.

Through this book, I am suggesting you take on a new role that may extend beyond that which you currently associate with grandparenting. I am asking you to become your grandchild's *nature mentor*. Rest assured that filling the role of nature mentor requires no special knowledge or experience. You don't need to have any formal education in biology, geology, or any other science. You do not have to know the name of a tree in order to help your grandchild experience its wonders-- just reach out and touch it, feel it, be with it. If you are inexperienced yourself, that is all the better; you can experience nature with the same wide-eyed wonder that your grandchild does. Whatever your life experiences have been, the gift of time has provided you with everything you need to excavate gems of wisdom hidden in the earth. Of course, a few basic truths about nature may help you start the conversation, and I will provide you with a few easy-to-understand fundamentals, as well as many ideas for fun things to do in nature (see Appendix). Ultimately, however, the direct experience of nature is most important.

Throughout much of the book, I address grandparents directly, but I intend to redefine the word *grandparent* in the widest way possible. In the spirit of the old well-known adage, "It takes a village to raise a child," I am really referring to any person who cares deeply about the next generation and the future of our planet. You might be a grandparent in the literal, biological sense, or you might instead be someone who interacts with children as a teacher, volunteer, or some other concerned member of the community.

I hope that this book can help create a better way of life on the planet. I have focused on grandparents because I believe that grandparents are an important resource for reestablishing humanity's faltering connection to nature and the planet as a whole. This connection can only be fully reestablished if children are taught the value of nature; they must be encouraged to step outside of the safety of home and the classroom, and away from the virtual worlds of television and computer, into the bright, vibrant energy of the natural world. *Grandparenting with the Wisdom of Nature* helps grandparents accomplish this in a comfortable and natural way.

I also hope this book will provide ways for grandparents and grandchildren to bond more deeply. Changes in our modern family lifestyle have, in general, led to the diminished participation of grandparents in children's lives. Through my own experiences as a grandparent, I have come to realize how important grandparents really are within the family dynamic, and studies of child development have confirmed that to be true.[i]

Of course, in an ideal world, parents would also participate in nature mentoring, but it is not easy for today's parents to maintain consistent contact with nature. Many households rely on dual incomes just to make ends meet, and many parents' time and effort is taken up by the practical matters of feeding, clothing, and educating their children. Even if they are environmentally aware and love nature themselves, young and middle-aged adults are often too "stuck" in the realities of our competitive, technological culture. They are left with little time to get back out into nature themselves, much less with children in tow. The current generation of parents grew up in a world rather disconnected from nature, and many may not know how to connect deeply themselves. Grandparents are the perfect candidates to step in and take up the slack, especially if they have reached retirement and have the time and energy to get back into nature.

You will see as you read this book that going back out into nature alleviates many problems faced by multiple generations in our culture. I am speaking especially of members of the Boomer generation, who are now entering their retirement years, and their technology-savvy grandchildren born at the turn of the millennium, known as Generation M. These are pivotal generations, and both can learn from the other in order to gain meaning and purpose in life. I know this to be true not only as a scientist, but as a Boomer grandparent.

We will all have to draw upon humanity's deepest sense of wisdom in order to make a truly peaceful and sustainable world for future generations of human beings. I believe that reconnection to the Earth will allow us to address these issues in the most honest and complete way possible. As we rediscover connection to nature, we can find reconnection to each other, as well.

The current older generation saw the rise of the environmental movement, and it is through our grand-children that it is likely to achieve its fruition. Within our lifetime, we witnessed the publication of Rachel Carson's landmark book *Silent Spring* and the establishment of the first Earth Day. Among us are some of the greatest pioneers in the field of ecology, but it is now time to grow environmental consciousness well beyond activists, scholars, and community recycling programs. Nature, and our ability to tap into its inherent wisdom, needs to be rewoven into the very fabric of life itself.

This cultural shift can happen naturally and easily if grandparents are willing to reclaim the mantle of elderhood. We need to reach back and embrace the ancient images of the powerful crone and the white-haired wise man. For too long, our culture has worshipped the attribute of youth and defiled the meaning of old age. Perhaps this reflects a misguided desire to escape the natural processes of life. Or, perhaps our fear of age is just a symptom of our technologically obsessed world where gadgets become obsolete almost as soon as they appear on the market. But human beings are not computers, and we cannot be replaced without loss of the most precious data of all--*wisdom*. To me, as a geologist, wasting the resources of elders seems especially foolish and shortsighted, considering that the entire history of *Homo sapiens* is merely a blink of an eye compared to the entire history of the earth. No matter what age, all humans are dependent children of Mother Earth, and we all have much to learn.

You may have your own important philosophical reasons to go out of your way to spend time in nature with your grandchildren. Of course, your grandchildren need not be privy to these more sophisticated motivations. For them, it is all about having fun, satisfying their innate curiosity, and spending time with someone who loves them. I would even suggest that the term "nature buddy," rather than "nature mentor," is more appropriate for use with children.

While I hold certain degrees and expertise that qualify me to write on this topic, this book is a personal story about my lifelong relationship with the earth. My adventures in nature actually started out as a means of escaping the less pleasant aspects of human circumstances and relationships. As I went deeper, I ended up learning just as much *from* nature as I did *about* nature. Perhaps John Muir, the naturalist who was among the first to advocate preservation of America's natural beauty, summed it up best: "I only went out for a walk and finally concluded to stay out till sundown, for going out, I found, was really going in."[ii]

At the end of each chapter in this book you will find a little anecdote designed to illustrate some point about nature, and show how grandparents and grandchildren can interact with nature. Although the scenarios presented are not necessarily taken literally from life, they are based on experiences I have had with children.

Through these little stories, you will get to know two characters especially well as they experience and interact with Planet Earth. The cuter of the two is a precocious little girl named Sophie. She is based on and named after the oldest of my five grandchildren, all of whom are very dear to me. Sophie, now eight years old, has begun asking some of the deeper questions about life. Watching her grow and develop from an infant to a school-age child has been a great joy for me, as it certainly would be for any grandparent. This joy has been accentuated by our times in nature together. Sophie serves as a kind of muse, inspiring me to write this book so that others can also experience the joy of grandparenting through nature. She will appear at various ages and stages of development. I hope I will have the chance to introduce you to my other grandchildren in future books as they grow and experience nature in their own ways.

It is significant to me that my first grandchild's name is Sophie, which is derived from the name Sophia, the goddess of wisdom. Sophie's little sister is named Sonia, which also means "wisdom." This coincidence reminds me that we, as the elders, are not the only conduits of wisdom. Children are the elders of the future, the sages and wise men of tomorrow. In the name Sophie, I hear the name of a goddess of wisdom in training.

The conversations Sophie and I have in this book are, for the most part, based on our actual discussions.

A few are hypothetical, based on questions that children are likely to ask. I include these to help illustrate how easy and natural nature-aware grandparenting can be.

I am the other person you'll meet, of course. The principles included here result as much from my own personal growth story as they do from observation of Sophie. People say that as you get older you enter your second childhood, and in many ways that is true. When you've lived enough decades on this planet, you eventually learn to drop the unnecessary pretentions of being a "grown up." Especially when interacting with nature, there is always something new and exciting to discover. When you have many years behind you and a small grandchild at your side, you cannot help but see the world through brand new eyes.

My nickname "Doc Rock" was given to me by my college-age geology students. I have come to truly value this name—after all, who doesn't want to be thought of by the younger generation as someone who "rocks"? But it means more than just that to me, as it reminds me of the earth that has been the foundation of my life, both literally and figuratively.

You will also be introduced to many experts and educators who are already making great strides to get kids back into nature. You will meet others who understand the important role of grandparenting and aging in our lives. Above all others, however, I am indebted to the work of Richard Louv, who coined the phrase "nature deficit disorder." In his best-selling book *Last Child in the Woods*, he demonstrates how lack of exposure to nature can lead to a wide array of physical, mental, and social problems for children. He links everything from attention deficit disorder (ADD) to obesity to depression to this problem. Part of the reason that kids lack exposure to nature, according to Louv, is that parents are simply too afraid these days to let their kids play freely. Now, thanks to Louv, the popular media are beginning to cover this issue. I wish to add to this conversation by suggesting that grandparents, as intergenerational nature mentors, are a safe and simple remedy for nature deficit disorder.

I would also like to note that I do not at all intend this book to be anti-technological in tone or purpose. I do question the tendency to rely on technology to the exclusion of interaction with nature, something Richard Louv refers to as "silicone faith,"[iii] but I do not at all think that technology is evil or undesirable. In fact, all sorts of technology, including e-book technologies, were used in the preparation of this book--search engines, word processing programs, a digital voice recorder, e-mail, and so forth. Technology as we know it today is simply a tool, different only in complexity when compared to tools used since the dawn of humanity. Tool use is as natural to humans as walking upright. Rather, my intention is to remind you that if you really want to "get connected," there is already a vast, miraculous natural network that is ready and waiting for you to plug into it. To give up that kind of connection for the digital kind is like trading diamonds for rhinestones.

Serendipitously, I did a little unintended time travel back into pioneer days during the preparation of this book. During the winter of 2010, the area where I live was blanketed by an unusually heavy snowstorm. Electricity was out for several days, and I was trapped in my home without heat and running water. I had to cook everything I ate over a fire in my fireplace, and I had to melt snow to bathe or flush the toilet. I spent most of the time huddled near the hearth, trying to stay warm in my snow-covered home. For me, the whole experience was a wake-up call, exposing my own dependence on technology and modern ways of life. There is nothing like a cold sponge bath in a home without heat in the dead of winter to make one appreciate how luxurious life has become.

Used well, technology has the ability to make our lives easier (and in my opinion, one of its best uses is to help keep us in touch with those we love). In fact, I encourage you to get over any lingering technophobia you may be experiencing, and start using these technologies, especially social media like Skype and Facebook, which will help you stay connected to your grandchildren, as well as with so many others who share the planet with you.

In reality, just the fact of being a grandparent is a natural marvel in and of itself. With the birth of my children, and now with the arrival of each of my grandchildren, I have been reminded of the wonderful cycle of life on this planet. Each generation rolls up like another wave breaking on the shore. What a blessing it is to share this planet with them.

It is my sincere hope that this book will help make you a more successful grandparent. Because people are living longer and healthier lives, we are able to fulfill our role as grandparent more vibrantly and actively than ever before. This is perhaps your greatest legacy to the planet and to the future.

In a way, now that human beings have been given the gift of greater longevity, grandparenthood is just now coming to its fruition as a normal human role. Children today can expect to have living grandparents in their lives, and it is up to us to live up to that expectation. Have confidence in the wise and wonderful person that you have become and know how desperately needed you really are, because indeed you are. Yet this is not a heavy burden or a difficult responsibility. All you need to do is get up and take a little walk into the woods with your favorite little someone.

Getting Back
into Balance

Wilderness is not a luxury

but a necessity of the human spirit.

--William Abby

In my earliest memories, it is hard to know where nature ends and I begin. When I was a child, my family lived on Long Island, only a block away from the Atlantic Ocean. My childhood was filled with the sights and sounds of the sea—the sandy grit between my toes, the rumbling crash of ocean waves, the penetrating warmth of sunny skies. The very earliest memory I have is of the two-and-a-half-year-old me sitting on the white sand beach, soaking it all in and reveling in the feeling of being alive and part of it all.

When I think of that little girl sitting there all those years ago, it is almost like glimpsing the essence of my real being, a part of me that is still looking, watching, and waiting to come out to play. Then, my sense of myself was only barely perceptible, like a light summer breeze upon the skin. It was as if my whole being radiated with aliveness that mingled with the sun and the ocean. Every seagull and sand crab was my friend; the waves curled over and crashed before my feet; the sand rejoiced with me, reminding me that I was alive as it tickled my skin. If that isn't bliss, I don't know what is.

Yet more and more we are denying our children and ourselves this kind of happiness. In the mid-nineteenth century, as the industrial revolution was just beginning to take hold of the human psyche, philosophers like Ralph Waldo Emerson and Henry David Thoreau warned us that the extraction of humanity from nature into the mechanical urban world would have dire consequences. As members of the American transcendentalist movement, they subscribed to a highly positive view of human nature, believing that humans possess within themselves everything they need to live healthy, happy, ethical lives. But life disconnected from nature, they believed, would disconnect people from their highest selves.

Thoreau retreated completely from urban life to rediscover himself in the context of nature. During his time in the woods of Concord, Massachusetts, he kept a journal that would become one of the first classic pieces of American nature literature--*Walden, or My Life in the Woods.* In it, he describes his motivation for returning to nature: "I went to the woods because I wished to live deliberately, to confront only the essential facts of life, and see if I could not learn what it had to teach, and not, when I came to die, discover that I had not lived." Disconnected from nature, people lived what he called "lives of quiet desperation" that led to corruption of body and mind.

Like Thoreau, I believe that time in nature is far more than a mere luxury to be experienced as part of a vacation. Rather, nature is a necessity for the health of the human body, mind, and soul. Introducing nature to children is as important as teaching them to read, to eat well, and to brush their teeth.

I first started to turn my focus toward the healing aspects of nature eleven years ago when the events of September 11, 2001 took place. Like so many others, I was shocked to the core, and I felt forced to look honestly at our human lifestyle. At the time, I was conducting a class called "Reconnecting to Nature," and I was struck by the fact that nature just kept on as normal, even while we humans felt like our world had changed irrevocably. Those events may not seem related to nature at first glance, but in reality the same paradigms that disconnect us from nature also divide us from each other, leading to hateful rhetoric and violent acts.

The unbelievable events of that day caused me to realize that I could not simply wait for lawmakers or industry leaders to do something about the lunacy of human behavior. I had to do something to make a change in the content and texture of our human world-because this was the world that my grandchildren would inherit. Furthermore, I knew that nature contained the power to help us heal from the wounds inflicted on that day, that Grandmother Earth was the best nurturer and healer of all. Thus, I hope this book will serve both grandparents and grandchildren, so that they may both, as Thoreau suggested, truly *live* life in connection with all the wonder and beauty that is this natural world.

The words of philosophers like Thoreau seem prophetic to the modern reader, as do the poems of Williams Wordsworth, who wrote of the "savage torpor" experienced by those living disconnected from the vital energies of nature. The social conditions and environmental degradation that these men witnessed more than 150 years ago is now, by most measurements, much worse. Every day there is another news story about global warming and habitat destruction. Even Walden

Pond, although rigorously protected by the Massachusetts' Department of Conservation and Recreation, has seen massive loss of plant and animal species.[iv] It is time for things to change, and your grandchildren may be the last chance for humanity to get things right.

But how do we get back in sync with nature? Is it too late for us? Actually, it is not as hard as it may seem. I have found that nature provides all the guidance one needs to live a balanced, happy life. In fact, it is impossible to live outside of the natural laws that are in place, although one can choose to resist or ignore them. These truths are actually quite simple to understand and to incorporate into one's life.

I will specifically introduce you to seven simple natural truths that are easy to introduce to children. These nuggets of nature's wisdom will guide you toward a more balanced way of life for you and your grandchildren. Here is an overview of these seven truths:

28

1.	**Everything is cyclical.** Everything that you see around you, from the water you drink to the air you breathe to the rock on which you stand, cycles endlessly. Learning to accept and embrace these cycles, looking for the promise they hold, is a key to personal well-being.

2.	**The world is a dynamic, changing place.** The earth teaches us that change can take place suddenly and dynamically, as in the case of earthquakes and volcanoes. From these changes, shifts in landscape can arise, providing new chances for life and growth.

3.	**Everything is connected.** The delicate balance of ecological systems shows that every strand in the web of life matters and that each strand affects the others.

Separateness and individuality are ultimately illusions.

4. **Everything follows a natural process.** The forces of time have slowly but surely brought forth increasingly complex forms of life. Humanity is simply another expression of that evolution. By learning to embrace the natural flow of life, rather than trying to control it, we can more easily reach our potential as individuals and as a society.

5. **To create is to thrive.** Nature is constantly creating. As humans, we possess brains that are especially well-suited to co-create with nature. Children and grandparents can tap into the source of life itself through creative expression.

6. **Nothing happens without exchange of energy.** Basic laws of physics tell us that

energy is never created or destroyed; it can only be transferred from one place to another. Learning to work with the flow of energy can transform our relationships with each other and with the earth.

7. **Diversity is advantageous.** Variety within a certain species allows greater chance for adaptation and survival. Diversity within human societies should also be embraced as a source of greater creative capacity.

If you are of a slightly cynical bent, you might ask, "But isn't all of this a little bit too sweet and sentimental? Can't nature be a mean and cruel place, one that's scary for young children?"

We may refer to the Earth as our "grandmother" because it is from her that life arose, and we continue to be dependent on her sustenance. Yet, nature is neither nice nor cruel. These are value judgments that we have foisted upon it from a narrow human perspective. Instead, nature operates neutrally, according to an intricate system of geological and ecological checks and balances. Within the protective bubble of these systems lie both our sustenance and our protection. As cruel as nature may seem at times, the planet Earth is in fact a perfect nursery of life, far more hospitable than any of our solar system's neighboring planets. When I refer to the planet as "Grandmother Earth," I do not mean to ascribe human characteristics to her, but rather to point out our ultimate dependence upon her bounty and protection.

Ironically, an unusually high number of traumatic natural events occurred while I was writing this book. There were earthquakes, tsunamis, hurricanes, and volcanic eruptions—many leading to great loss of life. These natural occurrences are undoubtedly disturbing, and certainly I extend great sympathy to anyone who has suffered as a result.

I personally experienced how unexpected nature can be when, during the final phases of this book's completion, an earthquake measuring 5.8 on the Richter scale hit the region in which I live. Very unusual for our area, it took me by surprise.

Experiencing these moments or watching the after-effects of natural disasters on television can be jolting as they remind us of the awesome power of nature, but really these events are only part of our planet's natural process of finding equilibrium. Yes, they can be disconcerting, but for me it is helpful to take the scientific point of view, asking how these events fit into the bigger picture of life. Also, it is important to remember that for every moment of drama that nature provides, it also provides tranquility and beauty in much greater abundance.

I am the kind of scientist who likes to get under the surface of things to see how they work. When I look at the world, I want to understand the underlying processes. I find that everything in the biological and physical world relies on interactive systems to keep functioning. A successful life, like a successful ecosystem, works in a similar way.

When I entered college, I had no intention of majoring in geology, or any other science for that matter. I took an introductory geology class by chance, intending merely to fulfill the general science requirement. As it happened, I fell in love with planet Earth, and the course of my life was altered forever.

I changed my major to geology, eventually earning a Ph.D. My dissertation examined a stream, and how it coped with urbanization. As I watched how the stream adjusted, I learned something about the universal processes of life, too. I learned to simply go with the flow of life without resistance. This became a guiding metaphor for me, teaching me to accept the changes of scenery as they come. With time, these observations led me to become aware of these seven basic principles of nature.

Science isn't supposed to be about emotion, but the truth is that I have fallen in love with nature, with all her fascinating intricacy and astounding beauty. During some of the most trying times in my life, she provided inspiration and insight. To me, she has become a living and breathing entity with a long history of trial and triumph. Through her strengths, I could glimpse the same in myself. As I began to understand the earth, I felt that I could begin to understand myself.

It has been said that children are natural scientists, so you could say that I am a child at heart. From the time babies are born they explore the world with their eyes, ears, nose, hands, and mouth, trying to understand the way the world works. It is this inquisitiveness that keeps the mind alive at any age, and no one is ever too old to explore and to learn. I invite you to embrace your own second childhood as you explore the world of nature with your grandchildren.

■■

For many days it has rained and rained. Sophie, her little sister Sonia, and her grandma are happy that the trees have gotten a nice, refreshing drink of water. They would like to play outside, but they've had lots of fun building forts with furniture and blankets in the sun-room off of the kitchen while listening to the rain hitting the roof. Sophie's grandma peeks out the window. Finally, the sun has begun to move out from behind the clouds and the birds have started to sing again.

"Mother Earth looks so happy!" Grandma exclaims.

Sophie and Little Sister trot up to look out of the window.

"Where is Mother Earth? I don't see anybody," says Sophie.

"Why, Mother Earth is everywhere! She is nature--the planet and everything on it."

Sophie thinks hard for a little while, her big blue-grey eyes darting glances here and there as she examines the scene outside. "But is she really your mother... like my mom is my mother?"

"Well, yes, she is... and she is your mother, too." Sophie cocks her head inquisitively.

Grandma chuckles. "Well, really she is more like a grandmother... our great, great, great, great grandmother who gave life to everything that has ever lived on Earth."

"Is she the birds' grandma, too?" asks Sophie.

"Yes, and the trees' and the flowers' and the mountains', too. Grandmother Earth takes care of everyone, just like I take care of you."

"Wow!" says Sophie, as her little sister bounces happily in front of the window.

Sophie's grandma laughs. "I think the rain has stopped for a bit. How would you like to go meet Grandmother Earth?"

"Yes, yes, yes!" Sophie and Sonia exclaim in unison.

The trio quickly put on their raincoats and boots. Sophie's grandma opens the door and off they go, hand in hand in hand, eager to uncover a world of adventure and wisdom.

●●●

☐

Grandparenting
A Natural State of Being

A society grows great when old men plant trees

whose shade they know they shall never sit in. Greek Proverb

As I look back on the moments of my life, I find that the ones spent in nature are the most genuine. In the natural world, I am able to drop the disguises of adulthood. Something inside of me expands and binds with the universe in ways that go beyond other happy moments. I have felt joy at a level that exceeds this only one other time--when my first grandchild was born.

I especially remember the moment that I took little Sophie into my arms and held her close. It is hard to describe—almost mystical. It was as if at that moment a ray of light penetrated my chest, into my heart, and into hers, and then out into the universe through time and space. Everything seemed to come together in that moment, all that has ever been and all that will ever be. The essence of life stretching out through the generations of living things on earth was tangible and seemed to connect all life on the entire planet as one. I have asked other grandparents about their experiences in that moment, and many reported a similar sort of feeling when holding their grandchild for the first time.

I've come to believe that there is some sort of vibrancy that underlies all life, and this is why I love nature so much. Through becoming a grandparent, I feel as though I have reached into the core of life and experienced it on a deep level. Giving birth to my own two children carried some of the same joy and feeling of connection, of course, but it was different, dominated by the laborious process of pregnancy and birth. The joy of becoming a grandparent, on the other hand, really took me by surprise. It was an experience rooted entirely in a state of being, the blessed state of being a grandparent and welcoming a new human being onto the planet.

I am so often amazed by the great blessing that is grandparenthood. We may take it for granted, but really it is a rare and special thing among living beings. No other animal lives so long beyond reproductive years, a fact that allows time and attention to be given to grand-children. Anthropologists believe that this offered great survival advantages to early humans.[v] Animal behaviorists confirm that the act of grandparenting is a uniquely human behavior. Only rarely do other animals even acknowledge their offspring's offspring.[vi]

I have now received this blessing five times in my life. With each grandchild, it is as if another cord of energy, perhaps what some call "heart strings," extends out from my heart to each of them, undeterred by time or space. In the case of my son's children, who live far away from me in Germany, I don't get to see them in person as often as I would like. Nevertheless, the connection is there, going beyond any limitations of geography and language.

Being a grandparent has undoubtedly deepened and strengthened my love and appreciation for nature. Of course, I have always felt a great sense of connectedness while in nature; that is what drew me over and over again to study and be one with it. And when I became a grandparent, this connection strengthened and deepened in indescribable ways. The passion that I once felt about environmental issues and the need to create a sustainable way of life became an urgent mandate that I could not ignore.

You probably have heard the ancient Native American proverb, "We do not inherit the earth from our ancestors; we borrow it from our children." If you are lucky enough to become a grandparent or a great-grandparent, I'm sure you feel the truth of this saying very deeply. Sharing nature with your grandchildren is not just a nice thing to do; it is a statement of gratitude for all that it means to be alive on such a wonderful, magnificent planet.

I worry about the world into which my grand-children have been born. I am concerned that we may have already stolen it away, that we may have already destroyed the thing that was rightfully theirs in the first place. Yet, I am hopeful, too. For all of our environmental abuses, life still exists in myriad forms and in almost every kind of environment, and it is not too late for much of the damage to correct itself.

Life is amazingly persistent. While there is no guarantee that life will be able to survive humanity's abuses, its complete destruction is only the worst-case scenario based on the notion that human behavior is absolutely fixed in its patterns. In reality, if we disrupt the Earth's intricate system of checks and balances, we will only harm ourselves. And, if we create a planet that is unlivable for us, we will undoubtedly take many more species with us into extinction. In fact, we have already eliminated many species and permanently disrupted many ecosystems through our carelessness. But life on Earth will probably find a way, with or without *Homo sapiens*.

Throughout the history of life on the planet, there have been various ages dominated by different life forms. First the single-celled organisms, then multi-celled organisms came along and eventually invertebrates were numerous. Then the vertebrates, such as fish, arrived on the scene. Reptiles, including the dinosaurs, became the most successful form of life on the planet, until they faced sudden extinction, which allowed mammals to proliferate and evolve into the different forms we see today. Today's natural world is undoubtedly influenced by the presence of humans, but in actuality we have only dominated the planet for a very short time compared to other highly successful species. Some say that the next period will be the age of the insects because they are the most diverse and adaptable life form inhabiting Earth. It remains to be seen whether or not humankind will continue to be successful or simply self-destruct.

In 2001, when I was teaching a class on reconnecting to nature and the tragic events of September 11 occurred, I sent out an e-mail to my students offering my sympathies and reminding them that it was more important than ever to go out into nature after a trauma of this sort. The next time I entered the classroom, I asked my students if they had done as I had suggested. No one had. Instead, like most people who witnessed the events, they stayed home, glued to the television. So I decided that we should do it right then and there. We all went outside for thirty minutes, quietly absorbing the sights and sounds of nature. When we came back, the students felt a great burden lifted, as they were able to share their emotions purely and freely. My personal epiphany was that the planet, Grandmother Earth, just keeps on giving, regardless of human affairs.

The birds kept singing, the trees stood strong, and the sun continued to shine.

When you bring your grandchildren out into nature, you help them become aware of the web of life to which they belong. Just by being in it, they will have the intuitive experience of their dependence upon that web. Pluck away too many strands and the web falls away. It can be woven again, but it will not be the same. To help our grandchildren's generation to realize this helps to ensure that the human strand will also continue. To allow otherwise is to steal from our grandchildren's grand-children that which is already theirs by right.

These days, many children are simply not experiencing the interactions with nature that filled me with such wonder and joy in my youth. Instead, it seems that we have replaced the beauty of the natural world with the thrilling but inanimate world of computers, televisions, and other gadgets.

Richard Louv began to investigate this topic when he noticed that his son was not having the same sorts of experiences that Louv had had as a boy. His childhood, typical of those growing up in the 1950s and early '60s in the United States, included unaccompanied playtime on the woods, where he fished for crawdads, climbed trees, and played games spun from his imagination. His son, on the other hand, spent most of his time indoors, playing video games and watching television. This initiated Louv's ten-year endeavor to investigate the consequences of separating kids from nature. His efforts resulted in the book *Last Child in the Woods: Saving Our Children from Nature-Deficit Disorder*, which drew attention to the importance of nature for our kids.

Louv found that there are a variety of reasons that kids are not playing in nature as much as they used to. Most obviously, nature is simply not as accessible as it once was. But more than that, we have generated a culture of fear that prompts parents to keep kids indoors.[vii]

We are afraid of accidents, bug bites, and the boogey man in the bushes, and, perhaps most of all, lawsuits. Thus, kids are left to seek adventure through "safer" means, such as video games and movies. The consequences, according to Louv and the many experts he cites, include all sorts of mental, physical, and social problems.

When I look at my oldest grandchild Sophie making her first forays into the larger world, I marvel at what she experiences. Where my school life was all about books and blackboards, hers is to a large degree digitalized. This is not altogether bad in itself. Actually, I am pleased to see the ways that it challenges her mind and allows the expression of her creativity. She has even used the computer to design her own picture book, something I would not have imagined within the capability of a six-year-old if I had not seen her do it myself.

The part that worries me is the extent to which computers are replacing live interaction, both with nature and with other human beings. One study conducted by the Alliance for Childhood which attempted to analyze the effect of computers in the classroom[viii] showed that little educational benefit is derived from computers. The only exception was a slight improvement in rote memorization tasks, such as when children learn multiplication tables. Still, personalized, one-on-one tutoring of students outperformed computerized educational programs in all learning categories, including rote memorization.

These days, kids' lives are regimented and structured. Often, after-school time is filled with organized activities like sports, dance class, music lessons, and the like. Even play time is a planned activity, as parents schedule play dates for their kids. In my day, there was no need to have playtime penciled in on the calendar. Kids just played because that's what kids do naturally. There was no need to be told what to do or how to do it. Our bodies got the exercise they needed and our imaginations were fully engaged, all without direction

49

from adults and without the need to plug something into the wall.

Sadly, our grandchildren are part of a stressed-out generation. Their worlds are full of competition, test taking, and little time for rest and relaxation. A recent study found that kids who have regular exposure to nature manage their stress much more successfully than those who don't, that kids who have easy access to nature are much more resilient when faced with difficult life situations, and they also have higher self-esteem. These children did not receive any psychological intervention or special training in stress management; just by being in nature they were intuitively able to develop the ability to transcend the experience of stress.[ix]

Nature was all around me when I was a kid, even growing up just outside of New York City. In those days, parents thought nothing of letting kids play on their own on the sidewalk. When I was twelve, my parents got me a little dog, a schnauzer I named Buttons. He and I would go to the beach alone and run along the ocean shore after school. We would jump from rock to rock on the jetties that protected the beach from the pounding of the waves. In a world like that, no one spoke of childhood obesity or nature deficit disorder.

I had so much more freedom when I was a child than my grandchildren do. I was allowed to ride my bike around the neighborhood unaccompanied, and there was no concern about danger. Our games were played outdoors--skipping rope, playing jacks and pick-up-sticks, and the like. Even when reading a book, I would opt to sit under the shade of a tree rather than sit inside. The natural world was our giant playground, and we engaged our imaginations with it, making our own toys from sticks, leaves, and rocks.

One wonderful thing I have discovered, though, is that you don't need to have an open tract of beach or a pristine wilderness in your backyard to bring nature to kids. In my home, I have lots of rock samples, fossils, and other natural treasures spread all over the house-- my decorating scheme, you might say. These objects provide wonderful opportunities for my grandchildren—or any kid who visits, young or old, for that matter--to interact with and discover the true wonder of nature. My fossils transport guests into a long-ago world, while a blue speckled bird's egg helps them glimpse the marvelous ingenuity and fragility of life. Richard Hammond, a host of a popular BBC science TV show for kids, says that all kids are "natural-born scientists."[x] I definitely agree, and to ignite their natural curiosity, it only takes *us* to provide the spark.

A friend let me in on a simple habit she developed that really brought children into the excitement and wonder of nature. She kept a simple birding book, the kind that helps you identify species in your region, on the coffee table, and marked the date beside the entry for a given bird anytime it was spotted in the backyard. The kids got into the act and made a point of identifying and marking the date for any bird they saw while visiting. They were especially excited when an owl came to visit the yard. They marked the date in the book, not really knowing if they would ever see it again. Then, to their delight, they did see the same kind of owl again. They went to mark the date in the book and discovered that the owl had visited on exactly the same date one year earlier. This simple act of observation corrects any assumption that bird behavior in the backyard is random. You can take this idea even further and more far afield: via internet chats and phone calls, you and your grand-children can compare the species seen in your respective regions.

I believe that nature has things to teach us beyond what can be conveyed through computer programs and books. I think there is an underlying wisdom in nature that guides the ebb and flow of life on the planet. These are the same natural laws that govern our lives, too. We may imagine that our man-made cities and the political systems that govern them are outside of nature's laws, but, in reality, they are not. By teaching kids about nature, and by letting them explore nature with their own hands and imaginations, you are exposing them to wisdom that can brighten their entire life, from childhood to old age.

I have spent some of the most difficult times of my life sitting on the banks of streams, pondering what the stream might have to tell me. On a practical level, I was there to study these watercourses scientifically. After all, that is my specialty. As a geologist, I study the life cycle of streams, tracing their birth at the tops of mountains to their ultimate return to the sea. But on a deeper, more profound level, I learned something far greater from streams than anything I could ever publish in a scientific journal, something beyond the facts and figures of scientific inquiry.

I have learned that there is a definite flow to life, both literally and figuratively. To resist this flow is to sink into stagnancy. When I am in sync with the flow, I remain vibrant and healthy in all aspects of my life. And when I ignore it, I stumble and my heart aches. We must help our children understand and live in alignment with this flow. There is no better teacher than Grandmother Earth herself.

If your grandkids seem different from you, almost too different to understand, please reconsider. One of the most important principles you can learn from nature is this: **Everything is cyclical**. Your grandchildren are simply at a different stage of the cycle. You can see yourself in them, and they can see themselves in you, if only both of you take the time to look.

You can point out the cyclical nature of existence to your grandchildren. Help them to notice how water endlessly transforms itself through its cyclical process, from ocean to vapor to rain to stream and back again to the ocean. Innumerable cycles happen inside our bodies to sustain our cells and to govern our life processes. Our brains rely on circadian rhythms to stay balanced and healthy. Likewise, we are dependent on cycles happening outside of our bodies, from the lunar phases regulating the tides to the carbon cycle that binds all life together. It is like a billion gears in a clock all working together, only a thousand times more intricate and complex.

In nature, everything you look at is part of a cyclical system. Indeed, there is a great deal of truth to the expression "everything that goes around comes around." Watch closely with your grandchildren as the trees change with the seasons, and rejoice with them at each step in the cycle. You might even try taking a picture of the same tree during different seasons of the year, making a game of noticing the changes that come with each season. Even the non-living world, like the rocks and soil beneath your feet, are in a constant cycle of generation and metamorphosis, as when lava is born from volcanoes, cools into rock, and then is transformed into soil through the forces of nature and time.

One potential problem with digital devices, including televisions, computers, and video games, is that they give the illusion that only one part of the cycle exists, as though the process of life could be stopped in its tracks. Youth is often treated in the media as something that must be grasped onto at all costs. The virtual world of most computer games is static and linear, treating life as a one-way trip from the beginning to a singular goal. This cultural tendency may leave some kids unable to accept the ups and downs of life, depriving them of the ability to see the grander scheme of all that is. By taking your grandkids out into nature, and by allowing generations to interact, they will have an unencumbered view of the cycles of life playing out before their eyes. There is nothing to fear or avoid about these cycles—they are as natural as a leaf falling to the ground or water vapor forming into rain clouds.

57

The stages of human life are not unlike the life cycle of a stream, which is why I have found so much inspiration in studying the stream erosion cycle. Just as we humans are born as small infants, a stream is born as a tiny trickle. It all begins high in the mountains when rainwater falls and accumulates beyond that which can be absorbed by the soil, vegetation, and rocks. When the stream is in its "youth," it is just beginning to establish itself, not unlike the child or adolescent who is trying to find his or her identity and place in life. Over time, the stream, working with and around the landscape it occupies, begins to establish channels on its way down the mountain. Not unlike the tumults of adolescence, the youthful stream is marked by fast-moving energy and drama in the form of waterfalls and rapids.

As the stream enters "maturity," it flows on more of a gentle landscape, like an adult who has found his or her stride in life. At this time, much "work" is done by the stream as it carries sediment from higher elevations toward the ocean. When the stream floods beyond its banks, it deposits this sediment temporarily on the floodplains, which become the fertile ground on which life can thrive.

Finally, the stream enters "old age," flowing upon a relatively flat and well-balanced landscape. Typically, the stream follows a meandering pattern at this point, slowly and gently flowing in graceful curves. However, the "old" stream can experience what is known as "rejuvenation" if there is sudden uplift of the region or a drop in sea level. The San Juan River's Goosenecks in Utah, for example, follow the meandering pattern of the older stream, but now erodes very energetically, thanks to geological uplift in the landscape.

Older humans, unlike the "old" stream," can choose what kind of landscape they want to follow. They could choose to meander through life or to invite the uplift that causes rejuvenation. Young people such as our grandchildren can provide just such uplift, filling us with renewed energy and vitality.

We grandparents are the keepers of wisdom. This wisdom, however, is not something that comes from us. Rather, it is something that comes *through* us. The wisdom is already there, within all the wondrous workings of nature and the cosmos, and it is the gift of time that has allowed us to cultivate it within ourselves. It is our prerogative to awaken our grandchildren to the wonders of nature so that they might gain even greater wisdom within their lifetimes.

■■■

Sophie and her grandma were taking a walk around a little pond when they happened upon a little turtle sitting on the bank. They stood watching as it slowly began to move. In just a few moments, it had slid silently beneath the water.

"I remember when I was a little girl I would visit my grandparents, and there was a lovely little pond with turtles in it. I even painted my name on the back of one once," said Sophie's grandma.

"You painted *Grandma* on the back of a turtle?" asked Sophie.

Sophie's grandma laughed. "No, no... I painted the name *Barbara* because that's my first name. I wasn't *Grandma* or even *Mom* then... I was just a little girl like you."

Sophie smiled and looked at Grandma, trying to imagine what she must have looked like as a little girl.

"I wish I could have played with you when you were a little girl," said Sophie.

"Well, we have our time together right now, and that is a very good thing. If I had stayed a little girl forever, how could I have become your grandmother?" said Sophie's grandma.

Sophie thought about it a little while then said, "I guess you couldn't have." She looked out over the pond and spotted three more turtles sitting peacefully on a rock on the other side of the pond. "Grandma," she asked, "do you think that turtle still has your name on it?"

"My turtle has probably lived its whole life by now because they don't live as long as humans... But I do remember how excited I was when I saw the same turtle the next year, a little bigger but with my name still on it."

"Can I put my name on one?" asked Sophie.

"Well... I have learned that turtles really prefer to be admired from a distance. How about if you choose one and give it a name?"

Sophie spotted a little turtle nestled up among the bigger ones. "There she is! The little one with the spot of yellow on her back. I'll call her... *Barbara*!"

Sophie's grandma laughed and said, "I am so honored! We'll be sure to visit her again to see how she is doing."

Sophie and Grandma said their goodbyes to Barbara the turtle and continued on their way, hoping to meet other friends who lived in and around that wondrous little pond.

Boomers

The Dynamic Generation

If future generations are to remember us with gratitude rather than contempt, we must leave them more than the miracles of technology. We must leave them a glimpse of the world as it was in the beginning, not just after we got through with it.

--President Lyndon B. Johnson

If you are like most grandparents of kids under twelve, you are probably a "Boomer," like me, born between 1946 and 1964. Much has been written and discussed about this particularly large and powerful generation. With all that's been said, have you ever wondered how we will be remembered a hundred years from now? Images associated with the Boomer generation tend to be youthful and brash: a young peace activist putting a daisy into the barrel of a soldier's rifle; countercultural celebrants frolicking in the mud at Woodstock; grungy, long-haired hippies dropping out of "square" society in favor of less restrictive lifestyles.

In reality, of course, time moves forward for our generation in the same way that it has for every other one. In fact, in spite of the Boomers' youthful imagery, we are likely to remain "seniors" longer than any other generation of humans ever to have lived on planet Earth. Boomers are enjoying longer and healthier lives than anyone before them, and because there are so many of us, the number of people over age fifty will soon outnumber those under fifty for the first time in human history.[xi]

As youngsters, the Boomers had an undeniable impact on the culture of Western society. We questioned cultural mores and demanded new ways of approaching life on the planet. In 1969, Theodore Roszak wrote a book called *The Making of a Counter Culture: Reflections on the Technocratic Society and Its Youthful Opposition*, and according to him, this generation, bolstered by its large numbers and youthful spirit, was the first to question, in large numbers, the relentless forward march of industrialization.[xii]

The ultimate effect of the youth movements of the 1960s and '70s remains debatable, however. To a large degree, they seemed to disintegrate due to the immaturity of the participants, devolving into a mass search for individual gratification and escape. In the end, for too many, being a "hippie" became more about style than substance, and Boomers seemed to settle down into a more conventional way of life.

According to Roszak, however, the revolutions called for by the Boomers in the '60s and '70s remain as a matter of unfinished business. In 2009, Roszak's follow-up book about the Boomer generation, called *The Making of an Elder Generation*, described the

67

revolutionary potential that still lies under the surface of this generation's collective psyche. Armed with the maturity gained from life experience, Roszak asserts that in our older years, we will shape our culture in ways that may offer true solutions to the limitations of our industrially centered society. In short, as Boomers enter the later years of their lives, they will exercise the deeper meaning implied by the word *elder*.

In her book *Crones Don't Whine*, Jean Shinoda Bolen recommends that women (and "exceptional" men) restore the ancient archetype of the crone. In the folklore of most Western cultures, the figure of the crone represents fully matured female power. In the matriarchal societies of long ago, she existed as the village wise woman, dispensing healing and guidance to all in need.

As "modernity" changed the structure of society, however, the crone's power became an object of fear and suspicion, as her image was distorted into that of a wicked and wrinkled old witch to be avoided and

68

despised at all costs. Our youth-obsessed culture continues to perpetuate this distortion through its refusal to celebrate the beauty inherent in the process of aging, especially the aging of women. By attempting to stay young forever, we are essentially denying our own right to the power of wisdom that comes with age.

Fortunately, the wisdom of the archetypal crone is one easily adopted by the audacious women of the Boomer generation, and it certainly may be as easily adopted by men who seek to regain the lost identity of the wise elder. Bolen writes of the crone:

> To be a crone is about inner development, not outer appearance. A crone is a woman who has wisdom, compassion, humor, courage, and vitality. She has a sense of being truly herself, can express what she knows and feels, and take action when need be. She does not avert her eyes or numb her mind from reality. She can see

the flaws and imperfections in herself and others, but the light in which she sees is not harsh or judgmental. She has learned to trust herself and know what she knows.[xiii]

The Boomers, coming into the full expression of their elderhood, are bound to redefine many things in our society. One of the most important of these may be humanity's relationship to the earth. The Boomers in their youth were the first generation to fully embrace the environmental movement, and as the imbalances of our interactions with the planet become more desperate, they will undoubtedly want to help reshape this aspect of the human condition.

Today's grandparents are already redefining what it means to be a grandparent. Being so closely identified with their youth, they are rejecting the stodgy image of yesterday's "Grandma" and "Grandpa" in favor of a more dynamic vision of elderhood. Since Boomers can reasonably expect to live twenty to thirty years beyond retirement, you can bet that they will want to infuse those years with a sense of meaning and purpose, qualities that have remained important to this generation from the beginning.

With new insights gained through life experience, Boomers now know that it takes more than happenings, demonstrations and sit-ins to change the fabric of society. Interpersonal relationships, especially with grandchildren, will likely be of primary importance, since this is where the heart of their elderhood can be found. Also, the need to heal humanity's relationship to the earth becomes profoundly personal when seen through the lens of one's own legacy. Elders must help their grandchildren recover a positive relationship with the planet because it is a birthright that must not be lost; to lose that is to lose ourselves, and could mean the demise of our species.

Modern society has disrupted the tradition of elderhood, just as it has disrupted the sense of community belonging for many people. For most of human history, elders have been a revered part of culture. Although in the past few people lived long enough to reach old age, those who did were regarded as special. Often, they became the figureheads of their communities as younger people looked to them to help make decisions and to guide them spiritually. As keepers of wisdom, they helped hold the center of tribal organization.

In their youth, some Boomers experimented with psychedelic drugs in order to reach states of enlightenment quickly and easily. As it has turned out, age may be the best "consciousness raising" experience of all. Roszak says it this way:

> Life in its normal course alters our consciousness more than any narcotic, especially if we are given the chance to reflect on our experience. The greatest transformations any of us undergo arise out

72

of the rhythms of ordinary life: the traumas of birth, the trials of adolescence, suffering serious disease, facing the loss of loved ones, confronting our own death. Aging turns many of us into totally different people. If we confront the experience with full awareness, aging can teach us what so many great sages have tried to teach: to be mindful of morality, to honor the needs of the soul, to practice compassion.

Conscious aging opens us to these truths; it is a mighty undoer of the ego.[xiv]

In the years since the Boomer generation first arrived on this planet, we have encountered (or been the cause of) an amazing amount of social change and turmoil. If nothing else, this generation is able to accept and embrace change as no other before it. Through the course of their lives and the history of their generation, they have exemplified one of the most important truths of nature's inherent wisdom: **Earth is dynamic; change is the norm.**

Many people try to avoid the truth of this basic principle, preferring instead a life free from anything unexpected. But changes, and sometimes dramatic changes, are part of life. The fool resists and fears the dynamic nature of life, but the elder sees the grander picture of things, and embraces the ultimate balance achieved through these events. Also, it is through this very dynamism that the forward evolutionary momentum of life takes place. In other words, without change, there is no improvement. Everything we are as human beings, including our intelligence and our adaptability, is the result of millions of years of shifting pressures.

In the time since I began writing this book, many major geological events have taken place, including two devastating earthquakes and a major volcanic eruption. Of course, the difficulties these events bring are real. In my case, my family was directly affected by the Icelandic volcano when my son-in-law became trapped in Germany for weeks because of the massive ash cloud hovering over Europe. This inconvenience, of course, is small in comparison to the pain and suffering experienced by those affected by the earthquakes in Haiti and Chile.

I do not mean to suggest that we should be cavalier about such events, but rather that we should gain an appreciation and acceptance of what these events mean on a larger scale. Rather than being taught only to fear and dread such events, children need to know that these things happen because the Earth changes just like they do. When an earthquake happens, it is just a matter of the Earth letting go of energy that has accumulated. As the tectonic plates move, stress builds up and must be released. From these changes, dramatic shifts in landscape can arise, providing new environments conducive to life and growth. The same is true of volcanoes, and it is through the outpouring of lava that new land mass is created and through eruptions that gasses are added to the atmosphere. In fact, the atmosphere and the hydrosphere upon which we depend for life formed billions of years ago from the degassing process of volcanoes.

When Sophie has a play date while I am visiting, there's a story about her mother and me that she always asks me to tell her little friends during dinner. "Tell the volcano story! Tell the volcano story!" Sophie would say. It is a story about a volcano that erupted near the hotel we were staying at in Hawaii.

It happened many years ago when my daughter was about fourteen years old. The management at our hotel on the Big Island of Hawaii announced to the guests that Kileauea, the nearby volcano, was erupting. Many of the hotel's guests became frightened and made ready to move to hotels farther away from the active area of the volcano.

I, being the eternal adventurer, decided to go in the opposite direction. I had to see the volcano up close. So my daughter and I left the safety of the hotel and began to hike bravely toward the volcano. Soon we could see the orange glow of the molten lava as it flowed slowly toward the ocean. This might have been exciting enough for some, but I wanted to see that lava as it met the Pacific Ocean. For me as a geologist, it felt like my daughter and I were getting a chance to see how the primordial Earth must have looked.

As the sun was beginning to sink toward the horizon, we finally spotted the telltale sign of earth begetting earth. In the distance we could see a faint fiery glow illuminating a spectacular plume of steam rising from the surface of the ocean as the lava flowed into the sea. This was a thrill like few others I have experienced, as I watched the energies of earth, fire, and water came together in sudden, dramatic fashion.

After observing the site for a little while, we turned and headed back toward the hotel. Soon I began to worry because it was getting dark, and I hadn't brought a flashlight. The lava rock was black and there was no moon, so everything before us was black. After a few more minutes stumbling slowly along in the dark, my worry turned into true dread as I saw a stream of red in the distance. I could see tomorrow's headlines in my mind's eye: "Geologist and Teenage Daughter Killed by Volcano." Fearing that we had been trapped between two lava streams and would soon be swallowed up by the superheated flow, my daughter and I sped forward, hoping that we were not too late to find a way out.

However, our panic suddenly turned to laughter as we saw what kind of flow we were really facing. As it turned out, the glowing red stream was, in actual fact, a parade of red taillights. The sudden mass exodus of vacationers from the area had resulted in a slow moving traffic jam, a calamity of a far less deadly sort.

I laugh at such a story now, but of course there are real dangers present in nature. I felt that trip to the volcano was a matter of balancing caution and curiosity. I must admit though that I really should have carried a flashlight and considered the possibility of new lava flows blocking our path. But this doesn't mean it was not worth the risk.

Sometimes even trained scientists miscalculate the dangers, as was the case for the two French volcanologists, Katia and Maurice Krafft. This couple was famous for their gutsy cinematography, often going to the edge of a volcanic eruption in order to bring home dramatic film footage. When asked about their dangerous habits, the couple insisted that they were unafraid. Yet, they were killed in 1991 along with several journalists when a Japanese volcano they were studying unexpectedly unleashed a cloud of hot, toxic gas and ash. Perhaps for them, as for me, a certain level of risk is acceptable in exchange for the soul-penetrating awe that one may experience during such adventures.

Often we humans expect that the earth is beholden to us, but in reality it is the other way around. We may be momentarily inconvenienced, and in rare cases endangered by natural processes, but in reality our very lives depend on the conditions they help create. All we can do is learn Grandmother Earth's lessons of gratitude and acceptance as we ride them out and make preparations for their inevitable return.

The same principles that exist in nature also exist within the framework of human life, whether we chose to acknowledge them or not. Just as the constantly changing physical world influences the biological world, our ever-changing human environment will influence who we will become. Sometimes we prefer to think of our society as unchanging and predictable, just as we may wish that the ground beneath our feet were absolutely stable and solid, without any possibility for unexpected events. Human society, like an individual human life, is indeed dynamic, ever-changing, and constantly transforming. In fact, things are changing now more rapidly than ever in our human sphere. You might even say we are living in "earthquake times" as the cultural ground seems to endlessly shift beneath our feet. Nature shows us that it is always possible to adapt, if only a little creativity is employed.

Having lived in an amazingly dynamic cultural environment from their youth onward, today's grand-parents may be the most surefooted generation of all, and because of the flux and pressure of our times, children are in need of the calming stability that their grandparents can provide. In helping children reconnect with nature, you give them a way of coping with shifting family dynamics, or other stresses of growing up in complex times.

Earth herself came into being through the dynamic action of cosmic debris colliding together in space, which generated heat that became the super-heated molten rock at earth's center. Eventually a crust formed on the surface and the Earth's core, tempered by the stabilizing effects of time and space, and provided the heat and chemicals needed to nurture life on Earth. Within the dynamic processes that give rise to change also lies the promise of equilibrium and balance that provides protection and nurturance for life on the planet.

The birth of our planet is not unlike the process of human cultural development—different people and ideas colliding to create the burning energy of passions within our core. If we can take the lesson from Grandmother Earth, we as a society can develop an elastic outer skin to achieve lasting balance. It may sound like a dreamer's dream, but for our grandchildren, facing the conditions of a crowded and threatened planet, it may be a simple necessity. By equipping them with the basic wisdom of the earth, you will be giving them tools to make positive choices.

Research has shown that people who value and honor elders also live longer, healthier, and happier lives.[xv] As we Boomers face the inevitable changes that come with age, we may realize that getting older is just another expression of nature's dynamism in action. And as we realize this in our own lives, we will be modeling the same for our grandchildren, who in turn will live happier and healthier lives. Now is our chance to create an elder culture that helps return human society to a balanced state in harmony with the principles that nature provides.

A large earthquake had just occurred the day before Sophie's grandma arrived to visit her granddaughters. On television there were frightening pictures of people being rescued from beneath the rubble. Some of these people were young children Sophie's age.

83

"Grandma, why do bad things like that happen?" Sophie asked, while sitting on the couch with her Grandma.

"I know earthquakes can be scary and even dangerous if you're unprepared, but they are really not a bad thing. Earthquakes happen when the crust of the Earth needs to release energy, like when you need to go run around outside."

"I think it is mean for the Earth to do that."

"Grandmother Earth isn't trying to hurt anyone. You see, many, many miles beneath the ground there is rock that is so hot that it is melted. On top of that there are slabs of earth called *tectonic plates*. When these plates rub against each other, move away from each other, or move past each other, energy builds up that needs to be released, which causes earthquakes," Grandma explained.

"Oh, I see...," said Sophie quietly, still thinking of the little children on TV. "Do you think we will have an earthquake here some day?"

"No, a very powerful earthquake is not at all likely where you live. They happen in certain places more than others." Grandma placed her arm around Sophie to comfort her.

"I don't want anybody else to get hurt," said Sophie quietly.

"I feel sad about that, too. Fortunately, we are getting better at understanding where and when earthquakes will happen and buildings are being built to withstand them better. Unfortunately, the people you saw on TV did not live in such earthquake-proof buildings."

Sophie nestled in next to Grandma on the couch, feeling a little bit better. She felt relieved, but understandably sad for the people who had been hurt.

Gen M
The Connected Generation

To the dull mind nature is leaden; to the illumined mind

the whole world burns and sparkles with light.

--Ralph Waldo Emerson

Technology has now become a full-time job for kids. In 2005, the Kaiser Family Foundation conducted a survey of 700 kids aged 8-18, all of whom were required to keep detailed diaries of their media habits. As it turned out, the average child in the study spent over forty-four hours per week engaged in media-related activity. In the moniker *Generation M*, the "m" refers to the indelible effect of media culture in their lives.

As you start to take your grandkids out into nature, you may find some initial resistance. This should be no surprise since the serenity of the natural world may seem dull to a child accustomed to the nonstop adrenaline rush of digital media. Even Sophie, who is now age eight, shows some resistance to the relatively quiet experience of the natural world.

Yet, it is essential that we find a way to get kids out into nature. Richard Louv, who coined the term nature *deficit disorder*, recently released a book called *The Nature Principle: Human Restoration and the End of Nature-Deficit Disorder*. In the book he cites a seemingly endless number of studies supporting the notion that *everyone*, not just kids, needs to spend plenty of time outdoors. These studies show that nature helps people both physically and mentally, and Louv suggests that lack of natural exposure is at the root of many of our sociological and cultural problems. In the book he refers to nature as "Vitamin N," and I agree that our Gen M could use a healthy dose of Vitamin N to help them grow healthy and strong.

It is important to approach the subject in a positive way. Ultimately, you want kids to turn to nature because they have learned to love it, not because you think they should. In reality, your grandchildren will need to be technologically savvy in the world of the future, so it would be a disservice to them to suggest that these things are in some way "bad" or "unhealthy."

Recently I went on a camping trip that illustrated surprising compatibility between technology and our experience of nature. I found out about the camping opportunity through www.meetup.com, a website on which one can find people and events in their own area that reflect their interests. I searched the word *camping*, and I found out that others in my area were gathering for camping trips. Since I prefer not to camp alone, I decided to give it a try. To my delight, I discovered that the people on the trip were both friendly and shared my intense love of nature. And to top it all off, we all decided to go out to dinner together at a restaurant we found through an iPhone application. In this way, technology can help us make connections with each other and actually accentuate our experience of nature.

I am concerned, however, when technology seems to detract from the direct experience of life. For example, on that same trip, I noticed many people spending a good deal of their time texting and chatting on their cell phones. I even found a group of teenage girls huddled around the only available electrical outlet in the campground's washroom, waiting for their cell phones to finish charging. The weather that weekend was perfect, and the scenery was stunning, so it is hard for me to understand such a choice. I am left to wonder if these behaviors are the result of informed decision-making or simply the force of habit.

Some have begun to wonder how all of this is affecting our kids. On the one hand, we want children to have access to all these technologies so they can be comfortable living and working in today's world, and the world of their adult futures. After all, in the twenty-first century computer illiteracy is bound to be as deadly to a person's progress as reading illiteracy was in the twentieth. But is it possible to get too much of a good thing?

Daniel H. Pink, in his 2006 book *A Whole New Mind: Why Right-Brainers Will Rule the Future*, argues that we are not providing our kids what they really need to succeed in the future. According to his theory, computers tend to develop skills in children that the computers themselves are designed to replace. For example, educational computer games are great tools for quizzing kids on multiplication tables and historical facts. However, the storage of vast amounts of facts in one's memory is no longer in high demand, now that information of all sorts is so readily stored on computers for easy access through the Internet and other databases.

Pink identifies six right-brain intelligences that will be key for our children's success in the future. Here is an overview of each skill and why I think nature serves to develop them:

- **Design**: According to Pink, the most successful products and services in the future will be the ones that take into consideration how the consumer and the environment interact with them. Designers are increasingly turning to biomimicry, looking to nature for examples of great design, such as new airplanes that incorporate elements of bird anatomy to make flight more efficient. I believe that time spent in nature from an early age develops intuitive understanding of the way nature works, something that can later be applied to creative endeavors.

- **Story**: Humanity has passed its wisdom down through myths and legends for centuries. Nature, with all its drama of life and death, birth and re-birth, creation and destruction, encourages children to see plants and animals as protagonists in the journey of life. Storytelling, more than relating scientific fact, is usually the best way to help young children understand natural principles.

- **Symphony:** According to Pink, people in the future, even more than today's workers, will have to understand complex relationships and work well with others in order to succeed. The natural world is all about connections between individuals and the environment.

- **Empathy**: Emotional intelligence will be as important in the coming century as logical intelligence. Children who learn to care for other animals and the environment will have developed the most inclusive kind of empathy.

- **Play**: Since having fun is critical for both mental health and creative processing, those who can engage in imaginative play throughout life will be at an advantage. As opposed to kids who participate in structured indoor activities, children who have ample outdoor time for "free play" will develop the best creative minds.

- **Meaning**: In a rapidly changing world, people of the twenty-first century will be challenged to maintain an intrinsic sense of purpose in life. Children exposed to nature gain intuitive understanding of life's greater meaning through the interconnectivity it demonstrates.

According to Pink, activities associated with the left side of the brain--mental skills like logic, math, and analysis--will not be as highly prized in the future as they are today, because we'll rely more on computers doing these things for us. Rather, the less clearly defined ability to process information through the creative and intuitive faculties of the mind, the primary right brain functions, will help a child stand out in the world of the future. These skills cannot be replicated mechanically, not even by the most advanced computers, and thus should be cultivated and valued more than they are in our current educational system, which tends to reward left-brain academic skills like mathematics and vocabulary acquisition almost to the exclusion of right-brain oriented abilities like music and art.

An obvious example of this left-brain bias is the SAT exam, which forms the foundation of college entrance standards in the United States. The test focuses primarily on mathematical and verbal ability, both left brain tasks, with little reward for creative thinking, even in the new writing portion of the test.

Nevertheless, school budgets for art education in the U.S. have been shrinking dramatically since 1997. Many schools have completely eliminated their in-house arts education programs, relying instead on outside contractors to provide occasional "arts experiences." According to Harvard University's *Ed.* magazine, many educators complain that this trend has negatively impacted students' ability to understand and communicate complex ideas, and they note that students' cultural exposure is almost totally limited to that provided by popular media. Nevertheless, it is almost impossible to measure the educational benefits of arts programs through standardized testing, thus the programs are continually downsized, especially during hard economic situations.[xvi]

I have found it easy to stimulate kids' imaginations when explaining nature to them. I might explain the water cycle by making a single drop of water a character, in a story that follows the drop from the top of the mountain to the sea and back again over the land.

I have found that Sophie too likes to tell stories, making up tales that represent her own level of understanding. Sometimes I will ask a question to get her to think about something, such as, "Do you think dinosaurs had to poop?" Wrinkling her nose up, three-year-old Sophie thought about it for a while. "I guess they had to poop, too... ew!" she responded. A while later, she concocted an imaginative story about Rexy the dinosaur who made a huge mess by pooping in the house. The moral of the story: "Don't let dinosaurs in the house because they will poop all over it." Clearly, a single question had generated a firestorm of creative thinking.

It could be that some playtime in an open field is all kids need to balance the dominance of the left-brained, technological world. Richard Louv in *Last Child in the Woods* devotes an entire chapter to the ways in which nature cultivates right-brain creativity in the young mind. He cites several studies conducted in Europe and North America that suggest that kids, when in a natural environment, are much more likely to engage in imaginative play. (For some examples of ways to stimulate kids' imaginations in nature, see the Appendix.) Louv goes on to give numerous examples of well-known creative people--Jane Goodall, Mark Twain, Thomas Edison, Beatrix Potter, to name a few--who considered their childhood years spent playing in nature to have been formative experiences that greatly contributed to their adult successes.[xvii]

You may find, however, that you have a hard time getting kids to take an active interest in nature at first. This is not surprising since computers, DVDs, cable TV, and video games offer them endless, fast-paced mental stimulation. These things are indeed fun and exciting, and when pursued in moderation they are not problematic. When allowed to become a constant feature of a child's life, however, they can become addictive.

Brain scientists have begun to refer to this obsession with digital media as "information addiction," and have identified the process occurring within the brain. Essentially, a strong dose of dopamine is released in the brain every time the senses are given a new piece of information. Dopamine is a highly pleasurable hormone associated with happiness and contentment. If you have ever had the experience of going on the Internet to search for one bit of information, only to get swept up into surfing the Web for a much longer period than expected, you have probably experienced this yourself. Blackberry users, noticing the time-wasting effects of Internet connection, sometimes refer to their devices as "Crackberry" because of this phenomenon.[xviii] In the brain, the iPhone was found to stimulate areas of the brain associated with love and affection, suggesting that people really do fall in love with their gadgets.[xix]

It's our duty as grandparents to help kids realize a more profound connection than that which can be experienced through technology. With or without a wireless connection, a fundamental truth remains: **Everything is connected.** In the natural world, there is a connectivity that binds all things together in ways the human mind can barely comprehend. This connectivity exists now and has always existed. To feel the wonder of nature is to sense the vast beauty of it.

I am sometimes truly amazed by the intricate interrelationships that exist in nature, sometimes appearing in ways you'd never expect. A severe case of poison ivy once made this especially clear to me. In the days just before I came down with the irritating rash, I had been walking beside the river, taking one of my typical nature hikes. My attention was continually drawn to a bright orange wildflower growing near the bank. I kept asking people I met if they knew what it was, but no one did. A couple of days later, I came down with the horrible case of poison ivy. I asked an herbalist friend if she knew any natural remedies, and she described jewelweed, a bright orange blossoming plant that grew in close proximity to poison ivy. She showed me a picture, and I recognized it immediately. To my surprise, I had been attracted to the very plant that would cure the ailment I had been harboring in my body!

My greatest concern for kids who spend so much time immersed in electronic media is that they are not being given the opportunity to experience *real* connection. Yes, they can chat with another kid in India and access a library on another continent. The Internet and other such technologies offer marvelous chances for interactions between diverse people. But if our grandkids have not first felt the vibrancy of our common heritage of life on planet earth, is the connection as deep and as significant as it could be? The earth is the ultimate porthole of connectivity, connecting us to every other living thing on the planet.

Daniel Pink insists that empathy, the ability to relate emotionally to other living beings, may be the most important right brain skill of the future. He notes as an example that Harvard Law School now offers a class entitled "Interpersonal Dynamics," which is intended to give its students the extra edge when dealing with people. This kind of intelligence allows individuals to comprehend subtexts present during negotiation and other sorts of conversation, a skill that is beneficial both personally and professionally. Pink argues the time spent engrossed by computers, television, and other personalized technologies deprives children of time that they would otherwise spend interacting with other human beings, thus undermining their ability to develop empathetic skills naturally.

Primatologist Franz de Waal, author of *The Age of Empathy: Nature's Lessons for Kinder Society*, argues that other species have a lot to teach humans about the art of empathy. Contrary to the popular survival-of-the-fittest view of nature, de Waal shows that compassion and cooperation are often key survival strategies in the natural world. Having made close studies of the great apes and chimps for more than 35 years, de Waal insists that we must learn their lessons soon if we are to survive as a species.[xx]

Having spent a lot of time with other grandparents, it is apparent to me that relationships between family members are among their greatest concerns. The family structure seems to be disintegrating, and kids are usually the ones most hurt by these situations. For many, technological entertainment offers a way to escape the difficulties of a changing family dynamic. As people, children and adults alike, escape into these virtual worlds, they easily lose sight of their connection to each other. A particularly grotesque example of this trend occurred in South Korea where a young couple starved their two-year-old daughter to death while obsessing over an Internet virtual reality game in which, ironically, they raised a digital version of the perfect child.[xxi] While this sort of extreme Internet addiction is not a concern for most people, in subtler forms it is epidemic.

In effect, our families' lives have been thrown off balance because the individual members them are retreating into their own digitalized cocoons. C. Margaret Hall, who believes grandparents have a "special mission" to bring balance back to the family, describes a balanced family this way:

> Balanced families have open, vibrant relationships that are based on meaningful, fluid exchanges among their members. Thus family bonds in balanced families are flexible but enduring, and the relatives interact freely and easily, both between genders and between generations. Balanced families are egalitarian in spirit, and relatives remain in contact with each other over time, whatever their immediate or long-term circumstances are.[xxii]

The family that Hall describes here consists of members who humbly acknowledge the interconnection between individuals. But as you know, real connection cannot be forced. You can't say to members of your family, "Let's bond!" and expect it to happen. The desire to connect with others must unfold naturally and voluntarily within the hearts of individuals. The natural world is an ideal place to nurture a sense of connection because it offers a comfortable, relaxing environment that demonstrates connectivity in an unobtrusive way. The interdependence of elements in the natural world is quite obvious, illustrating connectedness much more clearly than any lecture or textbook.

In my own family, I sometimes feel concerned when I see adults and children eat dinner together quickly and then each run off to their favorite, individualized electronic media. One evening, I decided to try something to get them to slow down and connect a bit more deeply with each other and to reflect on the day that they had just experienced. After dinner, I simply asked each one to share something positive about their day. Each told a different story, but I noticed that every one of their recollections involved interactions with people in their lives. Clearly, it was connection to people that mattered most to them after all. Sometimes we become so engrossed in the details of life that we forget how much people mean to us. Taking a moment of time to cultivate that appreciation for the "little things" can mean a lot to everyone involved.

Here is a fun, real-life story that can help kids understand how connected we really are on this planet.

In 1992, a freighter ship was crossing the Pacific Ocean when it encountered a severe storm. The ship was tossed so violently that one of the containers fell overboard into the ocean. Inside the container were thousands of small plastic bath toys. The container broke open and the toys began to float out onto the surface of the water. This was an unfortunate incident since it created yet another source of pollution for the already compromised ocean ecology. However, there was a silver lining to that cloud.

Over the course of the next decade, rubber duckies and floating plastic turtles began appearing on beaches on nearly every continent on the planet. Scientists began to track the location and movement of the toys, thus learning new things about the patterns of ocean currents on the planet. Because of that accident, they discovered that all the oceans of the world are intricately connected. For a little child dipping his or her toes into the ocean after hearing a story like this, it is not too hard for him or her to imagine that some other child in some far off land is doing the very same thing.[xxiii]

As children grow older, they can begin to understand, through observation of nature, that life is dependent on a healthy state of interconnection. You do not need to possess a great amount of knowledge to help illustrate this to kids, but a few interesting facts can be helpful. For example, you could talk about how flowers are dependent on insects to create more flowers. Or, you can show how even very distant locations are interconnected, like the South American rainforests of the Amazon relying on the wind to bring nutrient-rich dust from the Sahara desert of Africa.[xxiv]

Sometimes in my workshops I play a simple game with a ball of string to illustrate nature's connectedness. (It can be played with both children and adults.) First, I ask them to identify themselves as some aspect of nature, perhaps a rock, animal, ocean, leaf, bug, etc. The person holding the string asks, "Is anyone connected to me?" Then, someone who knows there is a connection must take the ball of string while the original person holds on to the end. For example, if one person is "animal," the person who is "water" might say, "You must drink me!" Everyone holds on to their portion of the string, but passes on the ball. After a while, a complex web of string is created as people discover that they are related to everyone else in some way or another.

More important than facts about nature, however, is the direct experience of it. Understanding the science that explains how an ecosystem works cannot replace the experience of *being* part of the ecosystem. This is the aspect that our grandkids are really missing when they choose to sit inside watching TV or playing a video game. To experience the wonder of nature is to experience the wonder of life. There is a vibrancy there that no biology book can ever hope to communicate. By taking kids out into nature, you are helping them experience what it means to be *alive* in the truest sense of the word.

I recommend that you take your grandchildren outside sometime after it has rained. Bundle them up in their raincoats and galoshes and let them go at it. Few things in nature inspire as much sheer joy in a small child as a few puddles and a rainbow. If possible, find a nearby stream channel and let them observe the changes that the rain has brought. Bring a magnifying glass and let them collect specimens to examine. Ask them what they notice. Chances are that they will notice the stream carrying sediment, which is what we geologists call the stream's "load." In fact, the stream is doing geological "work" as it erodes the landscapes and transports the load of rocks and debris from higher elevations to the ocean. If they haven't noticed that, you can point it out to them, and wonder about it together.

Allow them to discover the things to which they feel most naturally drawn and let them explore. For some it might be lizards, leaves, and snakes; for others it might be bunnies, sandcastles, and kite flying. The most important thing you can do is to be there and to help them uncover the wisdom that lies beneath the surface of these things.

There are lots of fun things you can do in nature with kids, such as the activities suggested in the appendix. But ultimately the most important thing is to simply *be* in nature, rather than always following the compulsive need to *do* something. In my adult workshops, I often lead an activity called the "Non-Naming Game" in which the participants are asked to avoid naming the objects in the natural surroundings. The object of the game is to simply *experience* the presence of the trees, the grass, and all the other elements in the environment. Through this sort of direct, non-analytical experience of nature, we can hope to experience the vitality that runs through and connects it all. Children, less burdened by the activity of the analytical mind, do this very naturally, when they are given the opportunity.

Our grandchildren are important to us because, well, they are our grandchildren. But I assure you that Grandmother Earth, if she could speak to us right now, would tell us how important we are to her, as well. The current generation of kids, Generation M, will be the ones who have to follow up on what we've done, and make some hard decisions about humanity's relationship to the planet. They may even be the last-chance generation in that regard. By helping your grandchildren learn to respect and be grateful for nature, you are helping them connect to principles that will inform the creation of a better, sustainable way of life on planet earth.

■■■

One day Sophie and her grandma were enjoying a beautiful day on the beach in Cape Cod. Sophie's grandma picked up a piece of drift wood and began to spell out Sophie's name on the sand: S-O-P-H-I-E.

"I can do that!" exclaimed Sophie, as she began to write her name in the sand with a stick.

"Very good! You write very well!" said Sophie's grandma, who then began to pick up little pebbles and arrange them in the shape of a B, for "Barbara," Grandma's name. Sophie came over to look at her grandma's creation. "Wow, that's nice!" she said. "I want to do that, too."

Sophie gathered a handful of pebbles and started to form the letter S, for Sophie. She found it a little hard because she had never made an S from pebbles before. But then she came up with a very clever solution. She first drew the letters in the sand with the stick, and then she placed the pebbles on top of the letters. Soon the name *Sophie* was spelled out in lovely little pebbles that had been polished by the sea.

Coming to Terms with Life's Processes

Climb the mountains and get their good tidings.

Nature's peace will flow into you as sunshine flows

into trees. The winds will blow their own freshness

into you and the storms their energy,

while cares will drop off like autumn leaves.

--John Muir

Our lives are a lot like water flowing through a stream channel. When we are young we are like the freshly melted snow rushing down the mountain to greet the warmth of springtime. Eventually the forces of life channel us into a given course as we follow gravity on the path of least resistance. Along the way, we encounter certain obstacles that churn us up and make the waters of life murky. Then, over time, our waters settle as we find a steady, balanced current in our lives. The sediment we carry with us from our traverses over the obstacles of life eventually filter out, ultimately bringing nourishment to that which grows on the banks of the life that surrounds us.

I was first inspired by the metaphorical meaning of streams when I studied them as a doctoral geology student. At the time, I was investigating how sediment is deposited along the stream bed as the water makes its way downstream. This happened concurrent with a very difficult time in my life, when I was dealing with divorce and the prospect of raising two children on my own.

I found myself relating very personally to the stream. (I was observing it so closely; in fact, that my professor was shocked by the great amount of data I'd managed to collect in such a short time.) The sediment reminded me of the personal burdens I was about to take on. My life seemed churned up, like the murky water, as I faced many difficult decisions, but I took comfort in the river's example: things would eventually settle and sort themselves out. It was as if the river were saying to me, "Take your time and allow peace to return." I also observed that the sediment simply dropped out when it became too heavy for the water to carry. The lesson I drew from that was that I too could only carry what I could carry--nothing more and nothing less--so there was no reason to resist. Pondering the process of sedimentation gave me hope that, with time, the waters of my life would run clear again.

In the course of all of our lives, it is really up to us whether we choose to go with the flow of life or resist it. Sadly, it has become all too common for people in our culture to resist the natural flow of life. People buy in to the unfortunate idea that a happy life is one that is static in its nature, one which delivers nothing but unwavering ease and happiness. Often, we look around us and want to cling to things just as they are, fantasizing that change can somehow be avoided. But as the ancient Greek philosopher Heraclitus noted so long ago, there is nothing permanent in the universe -- except change itself.

Resistance to change is especially pronounced in regard to the aging process. The media implore us to stay young at all costs, as though age were something to avoid and abhor. Billions of dollars are spent annually by consumers on wrinkle creams, plastic surgery, and other "anti-aging" products, all in the vain hope of escaping the inevitable.

In reality, aging is a great blessing which should be celebrated because it brings with it gifts that far outweigh its costs. As French philosopher Henri Bergson put it, "To exist is to change; to change is to mature; to mature is to create oneself endlessly."

Our obsession with youth may be even more costly to our souls than our pocketbooks. By denying our aging process and our elderhood, we pretend to take ourselves out of the cycle of life. In our technological world, we may have falsely convinced ourselves that we could live outside the processes of nature, and the results of this can be keenly felt in our lives as we disconnect from one another, from our planet, and from ourselves.

Grandparenting requires us to acknowledge the process of life. After all, no one would ever become a grandparent if the process of generational renewal were not in place. Any negative preconceptions you have about aging are likely influenced by the culture at large and rooted in the way your parents or grandparents or perhaps other older adults modeled aging for you. Through you, however, your grandchildren may have the opportunity to gain a more positive image of the aging process, which they too will eventually experience. By modeling a positive image of your own aging, you are helping your grandchildren accept a fundamental principle of nature: **Everything follows a natural process.**

Of course, aging is not the only process we experience in life. Childhood development is also a process, and a time of many significant changes. In that sense, older and younger people are well matched because both are encountering important transitions in the process of life. Both are learning to embrace new roles in life as they take on new identities and new ways of being. Grandparents are ideal candidates to demonstrate grace and acceptance in the face of these changes.

One of the most difficult aspects of the cycle of life is the reality that individual lives eventually end. A difficult topic for people to embrace at any age, for children it is especially traumatic as they move into their first awareness of human mortality, which often comes with the death of a grandparent.

You may find that your grandchildren notice your aging, and ask about your wrinkles or physical limitations brought on by age. In my opinion, observation of nature is absolutely essential for gaining acceptance of our mortality. Of course your spiritual beliefs may provide you and your grandchildren with comfort in the face of death, but nature allows us to place our wisdom within the context of three-dimensional reality. Through nature, we can see that while death may be tragic on the individual level, there is in fact great wisdom in Grandmother Earth's endless process of birth, death, and renewal.

Simple natural phenomena, like the changing of the seasons, serve as marvelous models of the ultimate value of natural processes. For a child, it is easy to wish that there were no rainy days to keep them indoors, and it is not unnatural for them to think that it's sad that leaves fall from the trees in winter. Grandparents, however, have a perspective that comes with time and experience, and thus are able to convey Grandmother Earth's greater design.

Arthur Kornhaber, in *Contemporary Grandparenting,* identifies being a grandparent as a developmental process in its own right.[xxv] In a sense, Kornhaber says, grandparents and grandchildren link the whole human life cycle together at opposite ends: the child receives, the grandparent gives; the child learns, grandparent teaches; the child is nurtured and the grandparent nurtures. Both are reflected in the other as grandparent sees where they have been and the grandchild sees where they are going. And of course, the grandchild becomes the teacher and the nurturer of the grandparent, in his or her own way.

Kornhaber contends that grandparents are critical to creating a sense of continuity in the human life experience. He writes:

> Continuity is attained and implemented by elders through a connection with others, especially grandchildren. . . by linking with those who are at the beginning of their lives, elders complete a full circle in life's journey and leave a bit of their "selves"

(wisdom, experience, personal example) in the minds and hearts of others. By so doing, immortality is attained.[xxvi]

Psychologists have long agreed that the human psyche undergoes a continuous developmental process. Abraham Maslow's "Hierarchy of Needs" theory attempts to explain the underlying motivations behind human behavior at various stages of life. According to Maslow, human psychological needs and desires begin with basic survival needs, and develop toward greater meaning and fulfillment in life.[xxvii]

Maslow identifies the following steps in his hierarchy of needs, beginning with the most basic: *physiological needs*, *safety needs*, *love and belonging*, *esteem*, and *self-actualization*. Consider how contact with nature could assist each step:

- **Physiological** needs involve the requirements of the body for survival and general bodily health.

123

Going outdoors contributes to physical well-being in ways that staying indoors cannot, providing fresh air, cardiovascular exercise, and stress relief. Developing the habit of outdoor activity in children is bound to contribute to better overall health throughout their lives. How wonderful it is to burn your calories by hiking through your nature conservancy, rather than walking endless laps on the school track.

- **Safety** is essential for helping children grow up to be confident and secure. In nature, children may encounter some things that seem frightening to them at first, but they can confront and overcome these fears as they understand more about how the world works. In learning the difference between a centipede and a millipede, for example, they can be taught which one is safe to pick up, and which one isn't.

- **Love and belonging** are essential prerequisites to happiness. These provide a sense of self-acceptance and worth. Grandparents who bond with their grandchildren while helping to connect them to nature show that they belong not only to a human family, but to the larger web of life as well. No matter what social situations arise, children raised in communion with nature know that they belong.

- **Esteem** is the need for self-respect as well as respect from others. Studies have shown that children who spend time in nature have a higher sense of self-worth and better problem-solving abilities. Perhaps this is because nature offers challenges that build a sense of confidence in all areas of life.

- **Self-actualization** is the process by which a person achieves their full potential in life. Nature helps both kids and grandparents embrace natural processes of growth and renewal that will bring this about.

All of these elements, when addressed satisfactorily, result in a happy and balanced human being. More and more, psychologists are recognizing the importance of nature in the process of personal fulfillment. An increasingly popular branch of psychology, called *ecopsychology*, theorizes that the human psyche is very much part of the web of life and that disconnection from nature is at the root of many mental problems.

Theodore Roszak, the same individual who wrote *The Making of an Elder Culture*, has been a leading advocate for the importance of nature for mental health. In *The Voice of the Earth*, he says, "An individual in harmony with his or her 'own deep self' requires not merely a journey to the interior but a harmonizing with the environmental world." In other words, to know the planet is to know ourselves.[xxviii]

In an article titled "Are We Happy Yet?" Alan Thein Durning, a senior researcher at the Worldwatch Institute, a global environmental organization, explores the possibility that humanity's search for happiness may be at odds with the needs of the planet. He concludes that the root of the problem is that we have falsely equated happiness with consumerism, believing that fulfillment comes through having plenty of money and a life of luxury. Unfortunately, lasting satisfaction is never achieved through the acquisition of these things, which inevitably create an insatiable appetite for more and more *stuff*. As a result, the resources of the earth are strained and people are less happy than ever. Durning's solution is to shift our consumer-centered culture toward one centered on earth stewardship.[xxix]

But how can we accomplish this shift? How can experience of nature compete with the undeniable excitement of the cyber world?

Fortunately, everything you need as a grandparent is already in place. At the deepest level, your grandchildren are already connected with nature and have a natural affinity for it. They may be distracted from nature by technical gadgets, and they may not have had many chances as yet to feel that connection, but it is there waiting to be developed. Biologist E.O. Wilson coined the term *biophilia* to describe humanity's natural love of living things, and he believes that this trait is something we are all born with.[xxx] Children, often attracted to animals, insects, and other natural objects, express this love for the earth very easily and naturally, if and when they are given the chance to do so. It is natural and fitting for you, the wise elder, to help them get the greatest level of benefit from this inherent attraction to nature.

The best way to help kids see their place within the processes of nature is to first make them aware of themselves. As they grow and change, you can point out how everything in the natural world is also changing. Some things change quickly, like a blossom opening and closing with the rising and setting of the sun; some things change slowly, like a mountain eroding under the influence of the rain and wind. Fast or slow, these processes are all part of the natural system that allows the continuation of life on the planet.

The processes of eating and digestion are a good way to demonstrate our connection to the natural world to kids. In a world of supermarkets and slick packaging, it might be easy for kids to take their food for granted, and to think very little about where the food might have come from. Much of the processed food that is marketed to kids is far removed from its natural state, almost to the point of being unrecognizable as having grown from the soil of planet Earth. Kids should know, however, that everything they eat, whether animal or vegetable, was once living. Life depends on life to grow and maintain itself.

In some schools that are beginning to embrace the importance of nature in learning, kids plant gardens and harvest the produce. By actually putting their hands in the soil and watering and watching the seeds grow into harvestable plants, children become witnesses to what food actually is—a gift from Grandmother Earth that nurtures and sustains us.

You can help kids see the importance (and roots! pun intended!) of natural food by having them plant some of their own or by taking them to your local farmer's market. You can draw a food web together. Encourage them to eat according to the seasons, and from local sources as much as possible so they can really feel the connection. Help them see that the foods they take into their bodies eventually become the cells that make up their muscles, bones, and organs. They will see that making healthy food choices is the best thing both for the planet and for their own bodies, and they'll feel connected to the earth.

Author Barbara Kingsolver and her family conducted an experiment in eating locally, an adventure that they chronicled in *Animal, Vegetable, Miracle: A Year of Food Life.* In the process, they discovered more about the reality of food production than they ever thought they would, from the politics that control our food production, to methods of organic farming. In the end, they also learned about each other and became closer as a family through meeting nature face to face.[xxxi]

Appreciating the processes of nature is often just a matter of slowing down a bit to watch and experience them. After all, you can't appreciate the inspiring sight of fledgling birds taking their first flight from their nest, or the majestic sight of a thunder cloud forming, unless you are willing to slow down and look.

Part of the problem for kids today may simply be the plain fact that they have too much to do. Psychologist David Elkind was the first to recognize something he named the "hurried child syndrome." He noticed that many kids participate in an excessive number of organized, scheduled activities and have little time for free play, outside on their own. According to Elkind, this results in kids' lacking imagination and carrying the burdens of undue stress. Not only that, Elkind posits that children also suffer from higher rates of depression too.[xxxii]

Perhaps it is time to de-emphasize competition among kids and inculcate more appreciation for what the ancient Eastern philosophers called the *Tao*, the natural flow of life. Lao Tzu, author of the classic Taoist text *Tao Te Ching*, said, "Nature does not hurry, yet everything is accomplished." In nature, all things find their balance, and we are the ones who choose whether to work with that flow or to resist against it. No matter what, we are bound to these processes, but we can choose to foolishly ignore their rhythms. The choices and the consequences are ours, and especially our grandchildren's.

Sophie was feeling sad when her grandma came to visit that day. She had just found out that her grandfather (not this grandmother's husband) had passed away. Sophie had seen goldfish and bugs die, and she had a friend whose dog had died, but this was the first time that Sophie had known any human being who had died.

"Grandma," she asked, "are you going to die someday?"

"Yes, someday. Eventually we all must die," Sophie's grandma replied.

"I don't want you to die," said Sophie.

"Yes, I know. But don't worry… It won't happen for a long, long time."

Sophie sat quietly for a while. Then she asked hesitantly, "Will I die, too?"

"Yes, but not for a very, very, very long time. You will spend many more years having fun, and changing, and growing before that."

"But why do things have to die? I don't like that," said Sophie.

"I understand. It is sometimes sad." Sophie's grandma got up and walked over to the window. "Sophie, come here for a minute. I want to show you something."

Sophie got up and walked over to the window. Sophie's Grandma continued, "Do you see that tree there, the one that has brown leaves, not green like the others?"

"Yes, I see it," said Sophie. "Why is it brown like that?"

"It too is dying. Does that seem sad to you?" asked Sophie's Grandma.

"Kind of. I feel sad that it's not green and pretty anymore."

"Yes, we will miss that. But that tree will now become the home for different birds and insects who need places to live. Eventually, it will fall down on the ground, break into smaller and smaller pieces, and become part of the soil, adding nutrients that allow other plants to grow. If trees and plants never died, nothing new could ever grow."

Sophie sighed softly and continued to look out the window. "Don't worry, Sophie," said her grandma. "Just keep all those memories of your grandfather in your heart, and soon you'll see all the wonderful things that can grow there."

Nature And
The Brain

Until man duplicates a blade of grass, nature can laugh at his so-called scientific knowledge. --Thomas Edison

I remember being a young girl, twelve or thirteen years old, reading *Gone with the Wind* as I sat under the shade of a beautiful tree. It was a truly blissful feeling, being totally engrossed in my book, while surrounded by nature. I felt like I was right there, on that old southern plantation, the sunlight shining through the leaves as the clouds drifted over my head. As I sat stretched out on the cool grass, I could feel the same connection to the land that I believe Scarlett felt for her beloved Tara.

These days we tend to think of education and nature as two completely separate entities. But in my mind, they are inexorably linked. Because we are natural beings, it simply makes sense to consider nature as an important foundation for learning. Louv's book, *Last Child in the Woods*, has led to some inclusion of nature in children's daily school experience. However, nature programs remain to a certain extent an afterthought in today's educational realm, usually relegated to occasional field trips and brief lessons on environmental stewardship. Grandparents as nature mentors can help take up the slack.

Another reason to study nature: it is absolutely clear that nature is wonderful for the brain. Research conducted by the World Wildlife Federation in 2010 indicated that unstructured playtime enhances student learning in every major academic subject area, and improves classroom behavior and concentration.[xxxiii] It's possible that outdoor "green time" may also be the best drug-free remedy for attention deficit disorder and other learning disorders of that type, which now afflict a significant number of children.[xxxiv]

Unfortunately, we are moving away from these advantages, not toward them, as humanity is being urbanized at an accelerating pace. Although we humans have spent most of our history in direct contact with nature, today, half of all the people on the planet live in cities. At the beginning of the twentieth century, only 14 percent of the earth's population lived in urban centers. This trend toward "citification" is expected to continue as our large cities expand into even larger megacities, with populations of 10 million people or more.[xxxv]

While city life certainly does offer mental stimulation, paradoxically, it seems that it may also be detrimental to brain function. After only a few hours on a crowded city street, the brain starts to lose memory and self-control. Researchers believe that this is the result of "cognitive overload," in which the environment presents a constant flow of stressful stimuli. To cope, the brain learns to turn off mental functions that otherwise help a person process elements in the environment. The results of this cognitive shut-down include lack of focus and emotional instability.[xxxvi]

Even a relatively small amount of exposure to nature can ameliorate this. For example, people dwelling in apartments with a view of nature have lower rates of domestic violence than those with no view. Psychologists Rachel and Stephen Kaplan theorize that nature has the power to restore equilibrium in the brain. The Kaplans' theory, Attention Restorative Theory (ART), asserts that nature provides "soft" stimuli to the brain without the negative stress factors of city life, allowing for better focus and a calmer emotional state. Amazingly, simple imagery of nature, such as photographs in a scenic calendar, can help produce this serene effect on the brain.[xxxvii]

Currently, I own a retreat business called Meeting Oasis, which provides organizations with a meeting space inspired by nature. Saturated with images of nature, the meeting rooms are conducive to better creativity and communication among attendees. When a group has a difficult situation or problem to solve, I recommend that we go outside and sit quietly for twenty minutes to see if any new solutions come forward. Inevitably, some new idea does appear. This also works with children when they need to find better modes of behavior or are struggling with some issue of growing up.

Unfortunately, the culture of childhood that I enjoyed in my early years, which took outdoor play for granted, is now largely a thing of the past in the Western world. Persistent fear of "stranger danger" has led many parents to limit their child's exposure to nature. According to one study, 82 percent of mothers of children age 3 to 12 don't allow their children to play outdoors due to crime and safety concerns.[xxxviii] Furthermore, researchers have documented the children are spending more and more time indoors, almost to the exclusion of outdoor play. One researcher, Mark Francis, referred to this as "the childhood of imprisonment," [xxxix] and another, Robert

Pyle, calls it "the extension of experience," a condition that undermines a natural sense of environmental stewardship.[xl] On top of that, the amount of time children spend playing in any natural environment has been steadily decreasing over time.

Some educational reformers advocate a longer school year and complain how kids in other cultures are spending more time hitting the books. While it may at first seem logical that more time in the classroom results in better cognitive functioning, research has clearly shown that playtime in nature is essential to full cognitive development. Consider, for example, the results of the following studies:[xli]

- After contact with nature, children with symptoms of Attention Deficit Hyperactivity Disorder (ADHD) focus better.

- Children with views of and contact with nature score higher on tests of concentration and self-discipline.
- Children who play regularly in natural environments show more advanced motor fitness, coordination, balance, and agility.
- When playing in natural environments, children's play is more imaginative, creative, and collaborative.
- Natural environments improve children's awareness, reasoning, and observational skills.
- Experiences in nature stimulate social interaction between children.
- Outdoor environments develop children's sense of independence and autonomy.

Yet most kids are spending more time behind computers and less time outdoors. In one case, a school district spent $200,000 to give Apple iPads to all of their kindergarten students.[xlii] Optimists suggest that this is creating a super-smart generation of multitasking brains, while others believe this is creating a dumbed-down world where people can only function in a mindless virtual context. Richard Louv in *The Nature Principle* suggests that there could be a third option—a "hybrid mind" in which the digital and natural worlds combine to enhance human senses and cognitive ability.[xliii] While an iPad may provide a fun and convenient learning tool, this is no substitute for what can only be learned through direct contact with nature and with other children.

The human brain has evolved to work within the context of the natural world as our ancestors knew it to be for generations. In other words, the human brain needs nature to thrive. Separation from nature may be robbing our grandchildren's the right to develop their full potential. Howard Gardner, a Harvard University professor of education, was the first to suggest that humans possess many different kinds of intelligences in different proportions in each individual. In his book *Multiple Intelligences*, he identified seven types of human intelligence, and later he added an eighth intelligence, naturalist intelligence, to the list as he extended his scholarly investigation of the topic. Although some academics criticize the theory, many educators have enthusiastically embraced the notion and are adjusting their classroom techniques to accommodate and develop a wider array of human intelligences.

I believe that grandparents should also be aware of these different types of intelligence, so that they can fully appreciate and accentuate their grandchild's abilities. As nature mentors, you will find many opportunities to build on all of the human intelligences as you experience nature together.

Here is a brief description of each kind of intelligence as it relates to your role as nature mentor:

- **Linguistic intelligence** allows a person to communicate effectively through language.

Children with high linguistic intelligence obtain vocabulary easily and are often precocious conversationalists. A more reserved child might express linguistic intelligence through a love of books or the ability to write expressively. As you experience nature with your grandchild, encourage them to talk about the world around them and what they observe, rather than simply talking to them. Nature can also provide the chance to introduce the child to simple metaphors and similes, such as "a breath of wind" or "snow glistening like sugar."

- **Logical-mathematical intelligence** allows us to complete mathematical equations, analyze problems through logic, and to investigate the world scientifically. When your grandchild asks questions about the world, you don't need to always give the answer outright. Instead, engage the child's critical thinking skills, and encourage them to find the answer through rational deduction. Allow very young children to count the number of seeds in an apple or the rings in a tree stump. With time it will become clear to them that nature as a whole is built on a rational, mathematical foundation.

- **Musical intelligence** is the ability to appreciate and perform musically. Some children have extraordinary abilities to play instruments and sing in perfect pitch, but even ordinary children have remarkable abilities in this area, all of which can be improved with practice. Studies have shown that children who learn to play an instrument do better in school across the-board, so it is well worth the time and investment to develop this kind of intelligence. Many activities in nature can help to develop this skill, as well. For example, you can let your grandchild listen to seeds rattling in a pod, identify birds hidden in trees through their song, or encourage them to hear the sound of wind blowing through the trees. There are an infinite number of sounds in nature that might be missed without the help of the nature mentor – the babbling of a brook, the faint rustle as one walks on the grass, the sound of the bird's wings as it lifts itself from the ground, etc. Help your grandchild discover the melodies and rhythms of Grandmother Earth.

- **Bodily-kinesthetic intelligence** coordinates the brain with the rest of the body. Athletic children are naturally talented in this area, but it is critical that all children develop this intelligence. Most obviously, movement of the body is essential for overall physical health. But in terms of the brain's development, it is also critical since physical movement activates all parts of the brain. Hiking

148

and exploring in natural environments allow for training of the body that cannot be accomplished inside of the classroom. Of course you will want to keep safety always in mind, but be sure to encourage your grandchild to explore in physically demanding ways such as scrambling over rocks, crossing a running stream by foot, or climbing a tree. These sorts of activities develop coordination and balance in ways that blacktop play simply cannot.

- **Spatial intelligence** allows humans to navigate and recognize patterns within physical space. Orienteering and cartography, for example, require high levels of this sort of intelligence. Gardner himself connects the development of this ability to outdoor play, since he himself was denied such play as a young child and now has difficulty in this area. You might also try investigating a new game called "geo-caching" in which participants search for an object using a GPS in a high-tech version of hide-and-seek. Allowing your grandchild to explore and discover large areas in outdoor environments provides them with the foundations of high spatial intelligence.

- **Interpersonal intelligence** allows us to understand other people so that we can engage and work with them more easily. People with high interpersonal intelligence are often considered to be highly charismatic because they know how to behave and communicate effectively. Although we rarely attempt to educate this intelligence in any academic setting, it is essential for success in virtually any career. It is the intelligence that allows us to see a problem from perspectives other than our own. The best training for interpersonal intelligence is one-on-one experience with other people. Empathy is an important component of interpersonal intelligence, so as a nature mentor be sure to help your grandchild relate to the feelings and experiences of others, including those of other living entities in the natural environment.

- **Intrapersonal intelligence** allows one to understand oneself emotionally and spiritually. With intrapersonal intelligence we build a sense of our own identity in relation to our inner feelings and desires. Natural environments, favorite places for meditation and other similar pursuits, have long been conducive to developing intrapersonal intelligence. Nature seems to encourage a sense of peace and connectedness that bolsters intrapersonal intelligence. As your grandchildren learn about the great outdoors, they will be learning about themselves and their place within the whole.

- **Naturalist intelligence** helps people interact effectively with their environments, allowing them to recognize and categorize features within it. This is the eighth intelligence that Gardner added after the publication of the original book. People with high naturalist intelligence have an intuitive understanding of natural laws. Its implications, however, are not limited to experience in what we call "nature," since natural law governs both biological and physical processes.

Naturalist intelligence is, of course, the type of intelligence most closely related to the theme of this book. In a video interview with BigThink.com, Gardner points out that we all use naturalist intelligence on a daily basis, even though it may appear as though we are no longer living in the natural realm. He says, "The neuron networks that evolved to help us get around in the savannas of East Africa 50,000 years ago are now being used in our consumer society."[xliv] In natural environments, children can develop their naturalist intelligence, averting the risk of the burnout that accompanies city life and multimedia overload.

I sometimes worry that our kids who spend so much time indoors aren't getting the chance to understand basic natural phenomena that would have been taken for granted a generation ago. I remember walking along the Potomac River when a teenage boy asked me how to "go around" the river. I told him that there was no bridge, but he still insisted on "going around" the river. It was as though he did not even really know what a river was or how it flowed continuously for a great length from the mountains to the oceans.

It is important to understand that the brain-boosting benefits of nature cannot come merely through abstract understanding of it. Most kids today spend more time watching videos that document nature than actually going outside to experience it. These documentaries are indeed beautiful, with vivid imagery and easy-to-understand information about how nature works. However, these videos often lend themselves to a sense of separation between nature and the viewer. This can only be remedied through direct, one-on-one experience of nature during which the child actually touches a leaf, smells fresh grass after rain, or feels the sun beating down upon her skin. In other words, all senses must be involved to fully activate the brain, not just the intellect.

According to Daniel Pink, author of *A Whole New Mind*, this sort of naturalist intelligence, a skill he refers to using the wonderful name of "symphony," will be in great demand in the future because it allows the brain to process competing information from one's surrounding environment. Pink believes that people in the 21st century, in order to be successful in the working world, will need to be able to discern significant relationships amongst the overwhelming amount of information available. Daniel Pink refers to the coming age as "The

Conceptual Age" because it will require people to understand the connections between diverse, and seemingly separate, disciplines.[xlv]

The so-called "graying" of our population may end up being a great blessing since older people possess great naturalist intelligence just by virtue of their lifelong experience. Neuroscientists have discovered that older people are able to problem solve better than younger people because they are able to take in large amounts of information and combine it and analyze it in ways that younger brains cannot. Researchers call this "broad attention span," a skill that differs from the youthful ability to focus on minute detail.[xlvi]

This ability is essentially the neurological foundation of wisdom, since it allows the older brain to consider a wide variety of information during the decision-making process, as opposed to focusing on just one or two elements as a younger brain might. Because this is a skill better suited to the older brain, grandparents can give kids a boost in naturalist intelligence, just by exposing them to this sort of thinking. Because nature offers limitless opportunities to demonstrate the power of connection through natural ecology, the outdoors provide the perfect place for this to occur.

In addition to its natural wisdom, the older brain is in peak condition in more categories than you might think. Barbara Strauch, in *The Secret Life of the Grown-Up Brain*, describes many discoveries that have been made recently about the mature brain. For many years, brain researchers thought that the brain declines with age, because they focused on tests of speed and memory. But as the research has become more sophisticated, it has become clear that many people's brains don't reach their peak until well after age 40, and sometimes not until they reach their 60s. Older adults seem to score especially well on tests of vocabulary, spatial orientation, and inductive reasoning, skills which happen to be especially well-suited to your job as nature mentor.

I sincerely hope that you will gain full confidence in your older brain—this will be essential for effective grandparenting. For too long we have insisted upon the inferiority of the older brain, as we joke about "senior moments" and other aspects of the aging brain. However, while you could say that a kidney or a liver will continuously decline in functionality through time, neuroscientists know that, without a doubt, the older brain does in fact get better with age in a number of ways. Yes, the young brain can process things quickly and retain new information more easily, but there are certain gifts that come to the brain only through time and experience.

This ability carries over into an older person's experience of nature. While the young brain might focus only on that which interests it, such as an interesting insect or a beautiful flower, the older brain is able to intuitively process the interdependence that keeps the ecosystem in healthy balance. Furthermore, the older brain will naturally make the connections between the events of our daily lives and the processes that guide nature as a whole.

While the older brain is indeed very well developed, you may still want to keep your brain as youthful and agile as possible. There are two important reasons why time in nature with your grandchild will help you ward off the negative effects of brain aging, like memory loss and loss of processing speed. On the purely physical level, it is well documented that exercise helps keep the brain fit, just as it keeps the body fit. Physical activity circulates oxygen to the brain by revving up the circulatory system, delivering the oxygen and nutrients needed to keep the brain in peak condition. Secondly, being with your grandchild as he or she discovers the world for the first time is bound to help you maintain a lively, engaged attitude about life, one of the most reliable predictors of longevity of both body and mind.

Another important way to keep the brain in top form is to consistently challenge it to learn new things and gain new experiences. Both older and younger brains need novelty in order to remain sharp and adaptable. The natural world, with all its variety, offers an endless cornucopia of experiences to feed the brain and keep it malleable.

In *A Whole New Mind*, Daniel Pink stresses again and again how the future will require highly creative, innovative minds. The human brain is especially well adapted to creative problem solving. In fact, neurologists believe that we never really stop creating, as we constantly create new interpretations and responses to the complex world around us. This feature, referred to as the "human spark" in a 2009 PBS series about the brain, may be the element that allows us to succeed so astoundingly as a species on this planet.[xlvii] Since the human brain is a veritable creation machine, it is a matter of accessing its full potential, allowing all of the various intelligences to blossom fully within the creative brain.

Naturalist intelligence and creativity are closely related because once you understand the principles of nature, you can adapt them in infinite ways to improve the human condition. For example, Velcro was discovered when a man noticed how burrs clung to his dog's fur. There is no way to say what other future innovations are still hidden in the natural world.

Encourage kids to look around and see just how ingenious Grandmother Earth really is. Encourage them to look at the way raindrops hit the windowpane. Ask them to contemplate why they stick and drip down in the way that they do. Then ask them where they think the water goes when the sun comes out and the puddles dry up. Encourage them to look at how a flower looks different in the day and in the nighttime. Ask them why clouds sometimes move quickly or slowly across the sky.

My favorite topic is dinosaurs because kids always love them and they are wonderful example of nature's creativity. Sometimes people mistakenly think of them as "failures," but they are actually one of Earth's great success stories. In fact, they were around for many more million years than humans, whose entire existence only equals a fraction of the dinosaurs' reign. And in the time that dinosaurs prevailed, they managed to adapt to just about every environment on earth. They even evolved to swim in the ocean and fly in the sky. And the story may not be over, since birds are thought to have descended from dinosaurs.

While creativity is what the human brain is all about, it is also what the planet is all about. You might say that Grandmother Earth is the most prolific artist that ever existed on the Earth, and perhaps in the universe, and we humans, gifted with our own creative powers, can look upon her creation as an endless source of inspiration. Creativity is essentially the ability to change and adapt, and adaptation is key to thriving on our planet. It is a fundamental principle: **To create is to thrive.** Thus, children and grandparents can tap into the source of life itself through creative expressions of the human brain.

■■■

Sophie was very excited to be going on her first camping trip with her grandma. She loved driving out into the woods and finding a space that would be like a little home for a couple of days. She could not remember ever sleeping anywhere but her bedroom, so this was a wonderfully new experience for her. The two set up a lovely little tent and made a lovely little dinner on a portable stove.

That night, Sophie looked up into the sky and was surprised to see all the stars sparkling overhead. "I thought they only looked like that in books!" she exclaimed.

Grandma laughed. "No, that's how they look. You just can't see them as well in the city because of all the extra light from buildings and and signs and streetlights."

Grandma pointed out a few constellations and told Sophie about some of the old legends after which they were named. Soon, dark clouds rolled in and hid the stars from view. While they were talking, a few drops of rain splashed onto their heads.

"Uh, oh. We better get in the tent!" said Grandma.

The two snuggled into their sleeping bags, listening to the sound of rain beating on the tent harder and harder. Soon rain began to seep into the old tent, dripping onto their sleeping bags. It became very cold and wet in their lovely little home. They grabbed their coats and ran out to sit in the car to wait out the storm. Disappointed, Sophie cried, "Oh, this is the most horrible night of my whole life!"

Grandma chuckled at Sophie's flair for the dramatic and replied, "It's really not so bad. Rain is very good for the forest, and it is a very natural thing to happen. When you go out into nature, you can't stop nature from happening! Plus, it's fun to sleep in the car, don't you think? It's a kind of adventure!"

In the morning, the sun was out again and the birds were singing. Grandma was able to buy a new tent that they put up right away, and they were able to dry their sleeping bags in the sun. Sophie was happy and smiling and laughing once again.

"Next time," said Grandma, "We'll be a little more prepared for the rain... This is how Grandmother Earth helps us learn." The pair enjoyed another night of camping, this time a little drier and whole lot warmer.

It's All About Relationships

Whoever you are, no matter how lonely, the world offers itself to your imagination, calls to you like the wild geese, harsh and exciting--over and over announcing your place in the family of things.

--Mary Oliver

One winter's day in Yellowstone National Park, I was lucky enough to experience a direct and intense feeling of connection to the Earth. It was very cold and snow lay very thick on the ground. My friend, a fellow scientist, was taking me on a tour, showing me geological and other natural features. We plowed through the deep snow on cross country skis, reveling in the amazing winter wonderland. Eventually, the freezing weather got to me, and I truly felt chilled to the bone. My friend took me to one of Yellowstone's less active geysers, and we lay down on the ground. Soon, I felt heat from the ground slowly penetrating my body, warming each of my body's cells one by one. I felt like Grandmother Earth was cradling me in her arms, giving me life and warmth directly from her core. I experienced a real sense of being alive and in the moment. As I recall that day, it seems ironic to me that as children are growing up, especially as they reach their teen years, adults often speak of the "real world" in ominous tones. We tell them how tough it will be and how they'll need to compete with all their might to stay on top. Usually what people mean by "real world" is the working world, as though an environment full of cubicles, desktop computers, office furniture, and stressed-out coworkers were somehow more real than anything else they might experience in their life. Encounters with nature, if experienced at all, are often relegated to vacations and holidays, times when people seek to escape from the constraints of everyday life.

Yet by isolating ourselves from direct experiences with nature, I would contend that our lives have, in fact, become less "real." Nature and the laws that govern her form the foundation of reality, and it is from *this* reality that all life springs. These natural principles guide the mechanisms that beat our hearts, grow our food, and allow our brains' synapses to perform their magical task of communicating. By pretending that we can remove ourselves from nature, we trick ourselves into believing that artifices of human society are somehow more important. More and more, however, we are coming to realize that we cannot escape our absolute dependence on Grandmother Earth.

The bond between humans and Earth may, in fact, be as powerful as any relationship between human beings. In the past thirty years, a new mental health paradigm based on *ecopsychology* has emerged. Eco-shrinks, as they are sometimes amusingly called, "believe there is an emotional bond between human

167

beings and the natural environment out of which we evolve."[xlviii] They have looked carefully at what underlies humanity's negative behaviors regarding our behaviors and have discovered that the basic psychology is that of the addictive mind.

The human psyche, according to eco-psychology, is as much part of the web of life as any biological organism. Thus, one way that psychological health must also be sought is through proper relationship with the Earth. Theodore Roszak wrote *The Voice of the Earth*, "...an individual's harmony with his or her own deep self requires not merely a journey to the interior but a harmonizing with the environmental world... We can not be studied or cured apart from the planet."

All of this points to something greater and far more personal than simply an environmental movement. Of course you can choose to work on the political level if you like, but how effective will that be unless people really feel their relationship to the earth in its totality? Can we expect to pass laws that instill true respect for the earth into people's hearts? In a way, taking a hike with your grandkids could be the most radical and effective of environmentalist statements. Boomers have always been a trailblazer generation that transforms the culture that surrounds them, and it's time for those of us who still have a burning passion for life to once again get out there to blaze the trail.

The media's negative portrayal of the "graying of America," works to instill a fear that this generation's aging will drag down the economy and stagnate our culture. In *Making of an Elder Culture,* Theodore Roszak rejects that premise, instead identifying boomers as the best-educated, most socially conscious, politically savvy generation of oldsters who have ever lived. Boomers who want to make their senior years meaningful and interesting will have, on average, a good twenty to twenty-five years left to live after beyond age sixty (and some of us, many more years than that). The question is what to do with all that time, to make it count. Roszak suggests: help make a whole new world. "The final stage of life is uniquely suited to the creation of new social forms and cultural possibilities," he writes.

Having an impact on our culture, however, does not mean we have to be part of a mass social movement. We can act individually. The simple gift of being a nature mentor facilitates a shift in our culture by allowing kids to understand directly their connection to the Earth. Everyday issues related to growing up, as simple as the idea of helping kids eat healthy, can help to accentuate the feeling of connectedness.

Sophie, for example, is one of those picky eaters would rather get by on a sugar high than eat her fruits or veggies. I have found, though, that helping her understand that food is the way Earth transmits energy to us really helps her understand the importance of it. It is not about doing what adults tell her to do, but about having the energy to do what she wants to do. "Food equals fun," I tell her, reminding her that the energy to skip, climb, and jump are dependent on the energy food provides.

Food can be seen as a kind of communication between the Earth and living things. Many of our illnesses today are related to our diet, a symptom of our imbalance and lack of connection to the natural flow. Food is actually a wonderful place to begin examining the wonders of nature, so next time you are eating with your grandchildren, take the time to really examine the amazing design of food. For example, cut an apple through the center and see the star shape in the center, or crack open a walnut and see how beautifully the two halves fit together. You might even recite a little poem or prayer with your grandchildren to commemorate your gratitude for Earth's bounty. Here's something I came up with to say with Sophie:

Thank you, Earth, for all this food.

It grows my body and lifts my mood.

So now that I sit down to eat

to sample all these tasty treats,

I want to show my gratitude

For all this fun and fabulous food.

And, of course, don't forget to sprinkle a little bit of love on the food, in whatever literal or figurative way appeals to you.

We need to really engage nature with our senses, not just our thinking minds. The tastes, smells, and textures of food are a good place to start. The five senses are the portholes through which we relate to everything in our world, and the places where all our relationships begin. To open these senses is to open ourselves to our full relationship to the Earth, and possibly to each other.

In *Reconnecting to Nature: Finding Wellness through Restoring Your Bond with the Earth*, Michael J. Cohen suggests that there are actually fifty-three senses through which we experience nature. These include everything from the ability to perceive sunlight on the skin to noticing hormonal fluctuation within the body. You may have noticed your own ability to perceive a coming change in the weather, or you may have had some premonition right before something was about to happen. Others might identify some of these abilities as "supernatural," but Cohen thinks that these are all part of the natural human psychology. Opening these up and using them, Cohen believes, can lead to complete wellness within the human body, mind, and spirit.[xlix]

Our schools tend to educate through direct instruction toward fact-based understanding of nature, rather than through direct, sensory experience. This is an important gap in education that you, the nature mentor, can help fill. As you walk with your grandchild, you are nurturing many relationships simultaneously: child and grandchild, child and earth, and self and earth. Helping kids view the Earth as a living entity on whom they depend does not necessarily require any lecturing or

173

instructing. Rather, it is matter of allowing opportunities for direct experience of nature.

I have learned a lot about these relationships through my business. Essentially, Meeting Oasis provides a place for groups of people from all kinds of workplaces to meet for effective dialog. What separates Meeting Oasis from typical conference environments is its connection to natural principles. Participants are not necessarily consciously aware of this, and they don't need to be. Rather, they are simply immersed and surrounded by natural elements, both indoors and outdoors.

When working with different types of organizations, I often find that they can benefit from an understanding of natural principles. For example, an important principle active in nature is: **Nothing happens without exchange of energy.** Furthermore, a basic law of physics, the law of thermodynamics, tells us that energy is never created or destroyed; it can only be transferred from one place to another. The same is true in human relationships—the flow of energy must remain open for the relationship to flow smoothly. Learning to work with the flow of energy can transform our relationships with each other, within organizations, and with the earth.

When I look at the organizations that come to Meeting Oasis with crisis situations, I can quickly determine that there is some clog in the flow of energy within the organization. In most cases, this energy blockage is in the form of communication breakdown within the team, but it could be monetary or in some other form, too. Highly functional organizations, on the other hand, illustrate natural principles through their relationships, demonstrating the critical importance of energetic give and take.

Nothing at all can happen in nature without the interplay of relationships. Most of these occur through the relationships of seeming opposites and contrasts—hot and cold, male and female, fire and ice, rock and water, etc. Internal and external forces are constantly at work on our planet—the heat and expansion of the inner core to the cold atmospheric exterior where space begins. Everything is in a constant mode of exchange—water erodes the mountain into the sea while forces deep within the earth push up from below.

For me, the disastrous fate of the Vajont Dam serves as a reminder of what happens when you ignore the realities of the natural world. In that case, three French villages were wiped off the map and more than 2,000 lives were lost because of human arrogance. The dam had been built in a deep gorge in the valley where these villages stood. During the design and construction of the dam, it became clear that one side of the gorge was weak and subject to landslide. Nevertheless, the engineers continued to fill the dam, sometimes emptying and refilling as they noticed the weakness in the structure of the land. At one point, a long crack opened up, indicating that layers of ground were shifting, yet this did not dissuade them. One fateful day in 1963, when the dam was near full, a huge landslide occurred in which tons of earth were suddenly deposited into the waters behind the dam. The water overflowed the dam in a giant wave that rushed down onto the unsuspecting villages below, destroying everything in its path.

In many ways, that incident is like a microcosm of the roulette game we are currently playing with the Earth's fate. Like the engineers who were so attached to the completion of their project, we continue to ignore the warning signs we are given.

Thinking we can control the process, believing we can bend nature to our will without hurting ourselves, is simple human arrogance. Our current mode of relationship to the Earth is too often a one-way street, which can never work according to natural law. Rather than working within the principles of balanced energy exchange, we have for too long taken an "I'll take what I

177

want" approach, and in the long run we suffer the consequences. This is undoubtedly the same kind of imbalance that undermines all sorts of human relationships, including family and societal relationships.

Our grandchildren have been born into a world where relationships are especially confusing and difficult. The cultural landscape is constantly changing, moral codes are being stretched and transformed, and diverse cultures interact like never before. Grandparents have an important role to play in providing relational stability in children's lives. Given their storehouse of wisdom, they are far more likely to truly understand the give-and-take of relationships. Even if they did not understand it in their youth, and even if they still struggle to fully express it in their own relationships, they have learned to some degree through trial and error.

In the past, people have relied on prescribed cultural roles to help them navigate relationships. These old paradigms may have made things easy to understand, but ultimately they are not in alignment with nature at all, where adaptation and give-and-take are the name of the survival game. In nature, when the environment changes, species get in sync with the natural flow, move on to another environment, or die.

Both nature and grandparents have a special role to play in helping kids cope and adapt to our rapidly changing world. And it is not really very difficult to succeed as a grandparent. The Silverstein study[i] listed these three simple elements as necessary to develop a strong grandparent-grandchild relationship:

- The child feeling **a sense of emotional closeness** to his grandparent
- The child **having regular contact** with his grandparent
- The child viewing his grandparent as **a source of social support**

The study goes on to state how valuable the grandparent is for modeling positive relationships. It concludes, "A strong emotional bond with the grandparent effectively models a healthy relationship... Imagine the very positive effect grandparents can have in their grandchildren's lives, if they're already receiving a healthy relationship model at home." Another study showed that the presence of grandparents in a child's life can help reduce the likelihood that maternal depression will be transmitted to the child.[li]

Really, relationships are the essence of beauty. As the old saying goes, "Beauty is in the eye of the beholder." To me this saying is true not only because the perception of beauty is an objective judgment, but because beauty is dependent on how things relate to each other. Beauty without the beholder, without relationship, is like the sound of one hand clapping.

Almost a thousand years ago, an Italian mathematician named Leonardo Fibonacci was the first to recognize that the natural world contains relationships that can be expressed mathematically. He recognized this underlying pattern when trying to estimate rabbit population growth based on a mathematical sequence. As it turned out, these numbers could be applied to many natural patterns. For example, the sequence can predict how branches are arranged on a tree and how leaves sprout from a stem.   Also, flowers can have vastly differing numbers of petals, from the one-petal calla lily to the thirty-four-petal field daisy, but the average number of petals for any species of flower always fits into the Fibonacci numbers pattern.

This pattern is seen repeatedly in nature—unfurling ferns, nautilus shells, weather patterns, whirlpools, and the shape of the Milky Way galaxy, just to name a few. In my home, I keep many different species of ammonite fossils that repeat the pattern perfectly and are a beautiful reminder that hundreds of millions of years ago these animals grew shells according to the same spiral equation. This pattern can also be seen in the human body as hair grows on a child's head and even in our fingerprints. And it is truly beautiful, is it not? When life seems hectic and chaotic, I personally gain great inspiration and comfort from observing these patterns in nature.

As a scientist and as a human being, I am convinced of the exquisite beauty of our lives within the grand scheme of things. Grandmother Earth is always speaking to us in her own kind of poetry. Our greatest legacy may be to remind our grandchildren how to stop and listen.

■■

It was time for lunch, but Sophie didn't want to stop playing with the pinecones she had found during yesterday's hike in the woods. Using sticks, she had given the pine cones legs with Play-Doh hands and feet.

She had also cut out shapes in construction paper, giving her pinecone dolls faces and clothes to wear. She had created quite a nice little pinecone family, and eating lunch was the furthest thing from her mind. Sophie's grandma called her once again from the kitchen.

"Coming!" she yelled back – without moving an inch.

A few moments later, Grandma appeared to fetch her for lunch. "Sophie, I've called you three times," she gently chided.

"I don't want to eat. I want to play!" said Sophie in a matter-of-fact tone of voice.

"Well, you have to eat," replied Grandma.

"Why do I have to eat? I'd rather play!" returned Sophie.

"Well… to play you have to eat," said Grandma.

"Huh?"

"That's right, Sophie. If you don't eat, you can't have energy to play. That's why food equals fun."

A few moments later, the two were eating peanut butter sandwiches on whole wheat bread that Grandma had sprinkled with little bit of love before cutting them into heart shapes with a cookie cutter. Sophie also enjoyed the carrot curly-Qs that Grandma had made with a vegetable peeler. Grandma showed Sophie a whole carrot with the green tops still attached and explained how carrots are a kind of root that absorbs nutrients from the Earth for the green plant that grows on top.

Later that day, Sophie and her grandma took a look in the backyard at all the living things that were busy eating or finding food. They saw a blue jay crack open a pinecone to get at the seeds inside, and hummingbirds buzzing back and forth as they took turns drinking from the feeder. They looked at the mulch spread out under the shrubs and looked at the earthworms helping to aerate the soil. A line of ants was busy carrying bits of leaf back to the nest. Sophie and Grandma stopped to look closely at a little green caterpillar that was busy

184

munching on a leaf. Sophie laughed at the way his bites looked just like the bites she made in her sandwich.

Natural History
As Cultural Legacy

A true conservationist is a man who knows that the world is not given by his fathers but borrowed from his children.

--John James Audubon

As I watch Sophie grow, I can see the image of the woman she'll become growing clearer in her face—in the line of her jaw, the curve of her brow, and the shape of her cheek. Looking into the eyes of your grandchild, you too may be able to glimpse the adult that lies within the face of the child. As we get older, it is natural to think about those we will leave behind and the legacy that we will bequeath to them. Thus, we prepare our estates, and we pray that our loved ones' happiness and prosperity will long outlast the days we have remaining on Earth.

Yet the word legacy means something greater than that which can be contained in wills and in family history. There is also a collective legacy we leave to our children and grandchildren in the form of the culture and world that we leave behind. Many years from now, when your grandchildren are your age, perhaps they will be taking their own grandchildren by the hand and leading them into a wider world. It is a beautiful image, but one that may also bring up feelings of worry. You may wonder, "What kind of world will it be?"

This sense of concern is natural because the world is changing so rapidly that it is hard to know what the world will be like in fifty or even twenty years from today. Once upon a time, people raised their children and grandchildren with the general assumption that the world would remain more or less similar to the one to which they had grown accustomed. But this is no longer the case. Today the world seems to be in a constant state of flux as cultures merge and new technologies transform our lifestyles.

The great blessing in this rapid change, however, is that the cultural choices available to our grandchildren will be much greater than they were to us, just as our choices have been greater than the ones available to those born fifty years before us. It is normal to become comfortable with what's familiar to us, but ultimately there is no reason to fear that which is new or different. In fact, it is a simple principle of nature that **diversity is advantageous.** Grandmother Earth is constantly demonstrating this to us through the wide variety of species and habitats available on this planet.

This principle is certainly true on the genetic level, since variety within a certain species allows greater chance for adaptation and survival. In terms of variety of life forms, the Earth is an incredibly diverse place. Scientists estimate that there are between 5 and 100 billion life forms on Earth, and only about two million of them have been identified.[lii]   In the deep ocean, new species with completely unique modes of survival are being discovered almost every day. Clearly Grandmother Earth allows all sorts of expressions of life to exist, allowing the most well-suited adaptations to emerge as the most successful species.

One thing that makes this planet so beautiful is the incredible variety of scenery and wildlife that it offers. Can you imagine how dull this planet would be if it only offered one type of environment, if it offered only pine forests or desert landscapes? And what if there were only a few hundred animal species? When we insist on ideology or customs that match our own, we are essentially asking for this same sort of monotony in the human realm.

Our cultural choices are also becoming very diverse, especially as technology allows for easy travel and communication. The planet is also becoming crowded as the human population continues to grow at an exponential rate. As people are able to migrate more easily, diverse cultures that once lived far apart are now often living side by side. Today, one in fifty people lives outside of their country of origin.[liii] Unfortunately, this has led to an increase in xenophobic thinking in much of the world. Nevertheless, change is bound to come quickly for all of us as cultures collide on what seems to be a shrinking planet. No matter how much you may value your particular set of cultural values and beliefs, humanity is moving away from focus on ethnic identity and national borders toward a more global sense of itself.

According to recent surveys, young people are much more willing than older people to embrace this inevitable trend toward globalization.[liv] The Pew Global Attitudes Survey shows that "Older Americans and Western Europeans are more likely than their grandchildren to have reservations about growing global interconnectedness, to worry that their way of life is threatened, to feel that their culture is superior to others, and to support restrictions on immigration." While the wisdom that comes with age is considerable, openness to new trends and the limitless potential and diversity of life is the wisdom of youth. Learning is never a one-way street, and this is the pearl that we can receive from our grandchildren as they experience the world with open eyes.

Personally, I decorate my home in artwork from all around the world, especially art that uses native natural materials. My favorite is a piece created by a resourceful West African woman entirely out of butterfly wings. These items help to remind me of the great, beautiful diversity that makes up both the natural and human worlds. When people from different cultures come into my home, I want them to feel honored and celebrated.

The grandparent's role in this increasingly diverse world is critical, however. While our culturally shifting world offers great potential, our sense of cultural stability will inevitably be harmed to some degree. The process of global cultural change is not unlike continental plates colliding on the surface of the Earth. Dramatic events will happen as a result—volcanoes will erupt and earthquakes will occur. Likewise, our grandchildren may live to see culturally cataclysmic events as people of differing points of view sort out just what kind of world this should be. Grandparents will serve as a source of stability at times when value systems and cultural identity seem to shift beneath our grandchildren's feet. We will be able to provide a sense of centered calm that comes from a long life lived well, a knowing that all things eventually return to equilibrium. If offered early in our grandchildren's lives, this solidity will follow them into adulthood, making them ready to face any obstacle.

The world may seem chaotic at times, but according to chaos theory, there is no "real" chaos. There is underlying order to everything. What appears to be disorder is merely new order coming into existence. Margaret J. Wheatley, an expert in organizational management, in applying the physics theory to people, succinctly sums it up: "Chaos is a necessary process for the creation of new order."

As grandparents, we can help young people learn to value and embrace the cultural seismic activity that they experience because this action creates new landscapes and horizons. In nature, without upheaval of this sort, the land would simply be eroded down to sea level by rain and wind over time. Instead, this interaction between opposing geological forces creates new land in an everlasting process of give and take. If you can imagine that the same thing is happening in the landscape of the human mind, then you can envision a beautiful future. Yes, there will be cultural earthquakes that upset the status quo, but ultimately we may end up with a human environment that is as beautiful as the Swiss Alps or as awe-inspiring as the Grand Canyon.

Diversity within human societies should also be embraced as a source of greater creative capacity. In A

Whole New Mind, Daniel Pink writes about how people's brains in the twenty-first century will need to demonstrate an ability he calls "symphony," the ability to make decisions easily and quickly when presented with a wide array of informational choices. Possessing this skill will allow people to cope with the diversity of cultural environments and will lead to global solutions that come from synthesis and cooperation, rather than contests of cultural chauvinism. In others words, the essence of human cultural creativity is diversity of mind.

Peter Senge writes about the desperate need for cultural change in his book The Necessary Revolution: How Individuals and Organizations Are Working Together to Create a Sustainable World. In the book, he provides a specific plan for individuals and organizations to move toward real change. He writes:

All too often, we humans live our lives as if evolution ended with us, as if the human was the last stop on the evolutionary train, as if all life on this planet has conspired to achieve the human form as its highest expression. Yet this tacit belief also contradicts the very idea of evolution itself, and indeed that of a dynamic universe in which evolution expresses, as poet Gibran said, "Life's longing for itself."

We are a young species who, uncertain of our niche, has very recently--in a mere second of life's day on earth--expanded to fill the world. In a sense we are like teenagers, full of enthusiasm and energy, and more than a bit confused. And, like every teenager must, we are about to discover that we are not the center of the universe, not even the center of life on this planet. We are but one of millions, and our merit depends not on our ego, but on our contribution.

Senge carefully points out that change must come from both individuals and organizations. All too often we blame the "system" without realizing that, unless we are living completely "off the grid" as true hermits, we are the system. To pretend that we are not directly responsible is nothing more than delusion.

Humans are unique in their level of influence over their own natural history. But what kind of future should we choose? The final answer to this question is up to many future generations of humans, but the initial societal choices are up to us. One thing seems certain, however. We must find some way to shift away from materialistic, individualistic obsession to find a way of living that is in harmony with the Earth and the rest of humanity. However, some may resist the notion of environmentalism because it seems at odds with our concept of self-reliance. There is really no need to abandon individuality, but there is a need to strike a balance between individual and collective needs.

Some people mistakenly think that our current cutthroat style of achieving individual success is actually in sync with natural law. In a process sometimes referred to as "social Darwinism," we often assume that the best

197

will naturally rise to the top of the system. Believing that endless, impersonal competition is the name of the game, people work tirelessly to attain material goods. "He who dies with the most toys wins," is an underlying mantra guiding much of human behavior.

The notion of "social Darwinism" is actually a great disservice to the memory of Charles Darwin, who first developed the theory of evolution. People sometimes mistakenly use the phrase "survival of the fittest" to describe Darwin's theory, but a more accurate term is "natural selection." The phrase "survival of the fittest" conjures up images of the biggest and strongest species using brute force to conquer those with whom they compete.

In fact, natural selection, the evolutionary process described by Darwin, is much more about adapting than about competing. In nature, all successful survival strategies incorporate the ability to adjust to the surrounding ecology. If the environment changes for some reason, a species must adapt or move on to a more suitable environment in order to survive.

In many cases, this includes mutualism, cooperation between distinct species, and even symbiosis, complete dependence between differing species. For example, many plants are dependent on insects and birds to spread their pollen to other plants, and in return they provide life-giving nectar to these creatures. Similarly, the red-billed oxpecker feeds on ticks imbedded in the hide of the impala, who benefits from having these parasites removed. In fact, species rarely make deliberate attempts to drive a competing species out of an environment. Rather, they find their own niches and unique strategies survive.

Watching Sophie grow over the past years, I have been impressed by how naturally compassionate she is. Of course, she has to be taught certain things about sharing and playing fair, but beyond this kind of socialization, she has a natural kindness and concern for those around her. For example, when we play a game, she is always very concerned and unhappy if the other person is losing, almost as much as when she is losing. And when she plays Twenty Questions, she can't help but give lots of hints to help the person out.

Dacher Keltner, psychology professor and author of Born to Be Good: The Science of a Meaningful Life, contends that positive emotions and relationships are as important to human health as good nutrition and hygiene. In his book, Keltner examines how humans are meant to be the most compassionate of all animals, a true "caretaking species." Even our brains are set up to care for others, and psychological and physical health deteriorates when the opportunity for nurturing is absent. Also, the fact that we live far beyond our reproductive age (i.e., to become grandparents and not just parents), suggests that these traits are essential to our success as a species.[iv]

It's quite likely that humanity never would have survived without our capacity for compassion. Our ability to form into small, cohesive groups must have sustained and protected our species for millions of years. But now human society has become much more complex than it has been for much of our history. In ancient days, we assured our survival through intense identification with a small group. But over time—and in a relatively short time in terms of the entire history of Homo sapiens--our sense of belonging has grown from tribe to village to nation. These affiliations are so powerful that we are willing to go to war and die to defend them. In today's seemingly shrinking world, we are taking yet another step, moving from national consciousness to global consciousness as we redefine who we are as a species.

Our current culture, with its emphasis on competition from the early grades onward, is out of sync with our natural capacity to connect and share with others. To me, it is obvious that our new global culture, whatever it may look like in detail, should draw upon our natural human capacity for goodness. The problem in the past has been that we reserve our natural goodness for those who share a particular identity with us, perhaps through religion, political affiliation, or ethnic grouping. But we can no longer maintain the sense of tribal separateness from others who share the planet. Perhaps it's even time to realize an even larger family, the one that includes all the life forms of earth...and even Grandmother Earth herself.

One of the oldest known life forms recorded by the fossil record are stromatolites, and although rarer than they once were, they can still be found living in colonies around the world. These ancient microbes demonstrate the same basic cell structure that would eventually give rise to all the life forms we see today. They first appeared on the earth 3.5 billion years ago. It was these simple creatures that broke the chemical bond of water, releasing oxygen into the atmosphere and making all future life possible.[lvi] We truly are one big family here on Earth.

That's why I believe grandparents working with children in nature are so important. It may seem like magical thinking to believe that exploring nature is somehow going to make kids better people, but research supports this notion. A University of Rochester study found that simple imagery of nature in office environments not only reduced stress but made employees more cooperative and community-oriented, while cityscapes produced the opposite effect.[lvii] Furthermore, older people are especially well-suited to teach emotional stability and positivity, since neuroscience shows us that the older brain is literally more "mellow" than younger brain.[lviii]

We must teach our grandchildren to value the precious rareness of our Earth. Like an exquisite dance, all this diversity is interacting, striving for perfect balance. We may begin to see environmentalism as a family issue, both because the choices we make now will affect our progeny for generations to come and because all life forms on Earth are essentially our extended family.

Whatever you do, please do something to connect to your grandchildren and to expose them to the feeling of belonging that comes through nature. While our changing world offers so much potential for growth, it can also create a difficult world in which to grow up. Grandparents can help provide stability when the surrounding world feels like it's loose sand beneath our feet. Author C. Margaret Hall calls this "the special mission of grandparents," being a critical factor in a new human being's life beyond the scope of parental pressures.

Many grandparents today complain that they don't get to see their grandchildren as often as they would like, due to geographical distance. With families scattered all over the country, and sometimes all over the world, visits may be few and far between. Becoming your grandchild's "nature buddy" is a simple way to bridge the geographical gap that may exist between you and your grandchildren. Even if you see your grandchildren very rarely, communicating with them about nature in any way can solidify your bond with them as you begin to orient them in the direction of nature. I encourage you to explore some of the video conferencing technology that is available, such as Skype and Yahoo Messenger. It's easier to use than you might think, and providing the visual connection is critical for Gen M kids.

Anytime you plan to chat with your grandkids, make sure you bring some treasure with you from the natural world that represents your geographical region—perhaps a sea shell, a cactus spine, a feather, a rock, a leaf. (Again, make your choices in an ecologically responsible manner.) Point out special features about the object, such as the textures or patterns they contain. Tell your grandkids where, when, and how you found the object. Then, place the object in a special box that they can look forward to investigating when they come to visit. You can also send it off for them to receive as a surprise in the mail. Have them do the same at their own homes, sharing their discoveries with you whenever possible. And, of course, when you go to visit make a big fuss about everything that they have found.

In these moments, really feel and appreciate the gift of being a grandparent at this particular point in time. In a way, now that human beings have been given the gift of greater longevity, grandparenthood is just coming into its fruition. Children today can expect to have living grandparents in their lives. Have confidence in the wise and wonderful person that you have become and know how desperately needed you really are. This is not a heavy burden or a difficult responsibility. All you need to do is get up and take a little walk into the woods with your favorite little someone.

One day, Sophie and her grandma decided to play a game of Twenty Questions. In that game, one person thinks of something and the other asks up to twenty questions in their quest to guess what it is. Sophie loves this game, and it makes her eyes sparkle with inquisitiveness and creativity.

Sophie started the game by saying, "Grandma, I have something for you to guess!"

Grandma responded, "Is it inside or outside?"

"Both!" Sophie shouted with excitement.

"Is it dead or alive?" Grandma continued to inquire.

"Both!" Sophie replied again. And then she added, "I will give you a hint. You and I LOVE it!"

Grandma couldn't at all guess what Sophie had in mind.

"It's NATURE!" she said, giggling.

Grandma and Sophie laughed together, and Grandma was so happy that Sophie felt the same way as she did about Nature.

Appendix

I. Nature Buddy Activities

Below you'll find many ideas for activities in nature. Of course, the activities you choose are really only limited to your imagination. Anything that lets kids engage their senses in nature while having fun will do. The key is to approach any activity with a sense of wonder, gratitude, and respect for the Earth.

It is not only a matter of what you, do but how you do it. Many more activities are available in the resources that follow this section, so please consult those sources for even more great ideas.

In the Backyard

- A Hidden Universe— Place a flat board on the soil and leave it there. After a couple of days, lift it up and see what sorts of creatures are taking refuge under it. See if you can identify any of them, with or without the help of a library book. Let kids draw pictures of all the creepy crawlies.[lix]
- Bird Watching— This old-fashioned activity has recently surged in popularity. Get a photographic birding guide, such as those published by Audubon, and then help kids start a "life list" to document all the bird species they have recognized. Also, help them to set up bird baths, feeders, or birdhouses. They will be excited to add to their list every time they visit a new environment.
- Camp Out—Set up a tent in the back yard and keep it up as long as weather permits. Encourage

kids to camp out at night and to play backyard explorer during the day.
- Bug Party—Drape a white sheet over a backyard fence and shine flashlights or a spotlight at the sheet. Observe the moths and other bugs that are attracted to the light at night.

At the Beach
- Tide Pools—Most beach areas have tide pools, so find out the location and the time when they are visible. You're likely to see different kinds of crabs, fish, and insects. Bookstores sell laminated fold-out cards that you can bring with you to help you identify specific animals. Show kids how to observe without harming the creatures.
- Pebble Sculptures—Let kids gather pebbles and rocks to make creative art in the sand. Encourage them to admire the natural beauty of the stones, and ask to ponder how the rock became so smooth. When the tide begins to roll over the sculptures, it's an opportunity to discuss how water helps to create some of our landscape's features.
- Time and Tides—Choose some marker, such as a stone, to mark the current high point of the water as it flows up onto the sand. Let the child report its current status to you throughout your day at the beach.

In the Desert
- Hot Rock Sauna—In desert areas with sandstone formations, try going out to lie on the rocks after the sun has begun to set. Let the child notice the solar heat still stored in the rocks.
- Sand Paintings—Collect various shades of sand in jars when you visit various locations. Pour them

into another small jar one at a time in layers to make a beautiful piece of art.

In the Forest

- Peek a Poo—Learn to recognize droppings from particular forest animals, like deer and coyotes. See if kids can guess what the animal eats by looking. Poke a carnivore scat apart with a stick to observe bones of other vertebrates, such as mice and birds, inside. You can take it home, remove each bone, construct the entire skeleton with it, and glue it on to black construction paper.
- Bark Rubbings—Bring some crayons and paper along with you on a hike in the woods. Unwrap the crayon, place the paper on the bark of the tree, and rub the side of the crayon on the paper to capture the texture of the bark. You can compare different kinds of tree bark when you get home.

On the Phone or Internet

- Nature Blog—Start a blog on an easy, free blog hosting service like wordpress or blogger.com. Provide the child with administrative access so they can post on the blog. Both of you can write about your nature experiences and share nature photos and videos. Share the link with family and friends.
- Show-and-Tell Video Conference—Set up a video chat service, such as Skype or Yahoo Messenger. Whenever you chat with your grandchild, show them something unique from the natural environment in your area, such as a leaf, seedpod, etc. Encourage them to show their own items, as well. Keep your items in a box for them to peruse when they come to visit.

In the Park

- Big Eye—Bring a magnifying glass with you to the park. Use it to look closely at blades of grass, tree bark, and the like. Use only with adult supervision, since magnifying glasses can be used to start fires.

At Bedtime

- Story Time—Choose nature and environmentally themed books to read to your grandkids. Many studies have shown that reading to kids makes a huge difference in academic performance. (See the next section for suggested books.)
- Remembering Nature—Have your grandchild recount the adventures of the day before going to sleep. This will help facilitate memory and establish the specialness of the day's events.

In the Car

- Nature I-spy—Play the traditional I-spy guessing game, but focusing only on natural elements that are within view. As you recall, one player chooses something to spy and then tells whether it is "animal, vegetable, or mineral." The other player must ask questions, up to twenty-one, until they guess what the thing is.
- Cloud Patrol—On long road trips, you are likely to experience many different cloud formations and weather patterns. Have kids notice how the clouds are moving and changing as you travel.

At Home

- Nature Journal—Let kids keep a journal chronicling their nature adventures. They can write, draw, or both.

- Junior Naturalist—Have kids collect natural specimens and keep them in a compartmentalized box. Be responsible about what you allow them to collect—never anything living or rare. Items should be numerous in the environment and easily replaceable, such as dead bugs, bird feathers, small bones, seed pods, and stones.

II. Recommended Reading for Grandparents

Get Out! 150 Easy Ways for Kids and Grown-Ups to Get into Nature and Build a Greener Future by Judy Mulland. Free Spirit Publishing, ISBN: 978-1575423357
Suitable for both grownups and kids over age ten, this book offers a treasure trove of nature activities and ideal for living a more eco-friendly lifestyle.

A Whole New Mind: Why Right-Brainers Will Rule the Future by Daniel Pink. Riverhead, ISBN: 978-1594481710.
Pink makes his convincing case that right brain abilities like creativity and compassion will be the name of the game in the future world that today's kids will inherit.

Last Child in the Woods: Saving Our Kids from Nature Deficit Disorder by Richard Louv. Algonquin, ISBN: 978-1565126053
Louv traces the consequences of children's lack of time spent in nature. He links many physical and mental problems afflicting children to diminishing contact with nature.

Animal, Vegetable, Miracle: A Year of Food Life by Barbara Kingsolver. Harper Perennial, ISBN: 978-0060852566

This book chronicles the year that she and her family vowed to eat entirely from local food production, which included raising a great deal of their own food. The charmingly written book offers a concise picture of our current issues with food production and its imbalance with the rhythms of the Earth.

Healthy at 100: The Scientifically Proven Secrets of the Worlds Healthiest and Longest-Lived People by John Robbins. Ballentine, ISBN: 978-0345490117
Robbins examines the lifestyles and diets of cultures whose citizens routinely live to be 100 or older. He concludes that a natural diet packed with veggies, along with a positive outlook, makes all the difference.

The Making of an Elder Culture: Reflections on the Future of America's Most Audacious Generation by Theodore Roszak. New Society, ISBN: 9780865716612
Roszak, one of the earliest experts to study the Boomer generation, makes the case that this large demographic still has the potential to make revolutionary change in our culture.

Crones Don't Whine: Concentrated Wisdom for Juicy Women by Jean Shinoda Bolen. Conari Press, ISBN: 9781573249126
This book celebrating the virtues of feminine aging will bring a smile to your face and help you embrace the power of the crone.

The Necessary Revolution: How Individuals and Organizations Are Working Together to Create a Sustainable World by Peter Senge. Doubleday, ISBN: 9780385519014
This book is a call to action, inviting us to join together for the sake of global health. If documents clearly how the materialistic world we take for granted is now coming to

214

an end, and it is time the create the kind of world we would like to live in now.

III. Recommended Reading for Children

Ranger Rick magazine   http://www.nwf.org/Kids/Ranger-Rick.aspx
Published continuously since 1967 by the World Wildlife Federation, this fun magazine educates kids seven and older about conservation and ecology.

National Geographic Kids magazine
http://kids.nationalgeographic.com/kids/
This is the junior version of the famous magazine with the gold border. It offers high quality photography with kid-friendly text.

My Big Backyard magazine
http://www.nwf.org/kids/your-big-backyard.aspx
Like Ranger Rick, this is published by the World Wildlife Federation. It provides kids ages 3-7 with nature education, especially focusing on animal facts. It also provides brain-challenging games and puzzles.

The Secret Garden by Francis Hodgson Burnett. Puffin Classics, ISBN: 978-0141321066
This classic children's book illustrated how nature can heal both body and mind through its heart-warming story of love and personal triumph.

The Dandelion Seed by Joseph Anthony. Dawn Publishing, ISBN: 978-1883220679
Chris Arbo's delightful illustrations bring to life this story of a dandelion seed's long journey to its resting place.

The Kids' Nature Book: 365 Indoor/Outdoor Activities and Experiences by Susan Milord. Williamson, ISBN: 978-1885593078
This treasury of activities for kids encourages them to do something nature-related every single day of the year.

The Earth Is Painted Green: A Garden of Poems about Our Planet by Barbara Brenner. Scholastic, ISBN: 0590451340
An anthology of nearly one hundred poems suitable for children written by famous poets, including Carl Sandburg, Shel Silverstein, and Margaret Wise Brown. All the poems contain themes related to the gift of planet Earth.

Listen to the Rain by Bill Martin, Jr., and John Archambault. Henry Holt, ISBN: 0805006826
This hauntingly simple and beautiful book celebrates the music of the rain.

Pond and River by Steve Parker. Eyewitness Books, ISBN: 0394896157
The high quality photographs in this volume bring stream ecology to life for kids of middle school age. It's the next best thing to being there in person.

A Log's Life by Wendy Pfeffer. Simon and Schuster Books for Young Readers, ISBN: 0689806361
Illustrated using a unique collage technique, this inspiring book educates readers about the important ecological role a tree plays throughout its lifespan, from seedling to decaying log.

The Giving Tree by Shel Silverstein. Harpercollins Juvenile Books, ISBN: 0060256656
This is the classic story of a tree who gives unconditionally to the boy who enjoys her apples and her shade. It becomes a subtle parable about humanity's

relationship to the Earth, who gives to us endlessly without the need for love in return.

IV. Internet Resources
Nature for Kids http://natureforkids.net/
This blog encourages families with young children to get out there and experience the natural world together. The most charming features of this blog are the cute videos and photos, which will inspire little ones to go out and play.

Kids Discover Nature
http://www.kidsdiscovernature.com/
This blog provides nature activities and environmental education for kids from an ecologist and environmental scientist.

Children and Nature Network
http://www.childrenandnature.org/
This is a storehouse of everything related to kids and nature. You can find updates about research related to the topic, and you can connect to people with similar interests.

National Wildlife Federation http://www.nwf.org/Get-Outside/Be-Out-There.aspx
The NWF's Be Out There campaign provides plenty of information for adults working with children in nature, including downloadable content. It also helps keep people aware of related political developments.

*Wild Birds Unlimited_* http://www.wbu.com
This is an especially great resource if your grandchild is a budding birder, but it also has lots of other great nature

activities available on their "Pathways to Nature for Kids" page.

Backyard Mama http://www.backyardmama.com/
This former elementary school teacher now offers nature-based childcare in her back yard. She is also a certified yoga instructor and stresses the importance of movement for children. In this blog she offers numerous activities that can be done right in your backyard.

Go Explore Nature http://goexplorenature.blogspot.com/
A Los Angeles area mom blogs about nature adventures with her two small sons. It includes lots of great ideas for fun in various environments.

Handbook   of   Nature   Study
http://handbookofnaturestudy.blogspot.com/
This is a simple blog started by a family about their experiences in nature that has gained some popularity. It includes many "Outdoor Hour Challenges," fun nature activities that don't take much time.

RichardLouv.com http://richardlouv.com/children-nature-resources
The site provides every think you might want to know about Louv, author of *Last Child in the Woods*. It provides a wealth of nature activities, new information supporting his theory, and recent articles written by Louv.

About The Author

Dr. Barbara Frank has devoted her career to experiential education, adult learning, senior government management, and organizational consulting. All of these roles are linked by her understanding of human behavior and natural systems. In 1997, Dr. Frank created Meeting Oasis, a venue with a naturally supportive environment for strategic meetings and retreats (www. MeetingOasis.) Over the years, she has gained reputation for her nature-based team performance training and for the hospitality she offers to her clients and to other consultants and trainers. She currently focuses on helping adults and children bond through nature with her website on dinosaurs.

To Contact Barbara Frank

Dr. Frank is available workshops, trips and public speaking engagements.
www.GrandparentsIntoNature.com
barbarajoycefrank@gmail.com

Acknowledgments

Many thanks to my friends Larry Rosenberg, Jayne Cantor, Gini Quante, BJ Scott-Turner, Nancy Rome, Paul and Paula Weisshaar and Rebecca Weissman for their encouragement, advice and support while writing this book.

My gratitude to Nicole Dean and Jill Bailin for their special assistance in bringing this book to fruition.

Special thanks to my muse, my granddaughter Sophie. Her birth made me a grandmother for the first time and being with her is always a joy and inspiration.

References

[i] AARP. *The Grandparent Study.* www.researchaarp.com, 2002.

[ii] Muir, John. *John Muir, John of the Mountains: The Unpublished Journals of John Muir.* L.M. Wolfe, 1938

[iii] Louv, Richard. *Last Child in the Woods: Saving Our Children from Nature Deficit Disorder.* Chapel Hill, NC: Algonquin, 2007. 136-7.

[iv] Maynard, W. Barksdale. *Walden Pond: A History.* Oxford University Press, 2005.

[v] Lahdenperä, M., et al. "Fitness Benefits of Prolonged Post-reproductive Lifespan in Women." *Nature.* (2004). 428. 178–181.

[vi] Choi, Charles Q. "Birds Act Like Grandparents." Livescience.com. January 8, 2008

[vii] Louv, Richard. *Last Child in the Woods: Saving Our Children from Nature Deficit Disorder.* Chapel Hill, NC: Algonquin, 2007. 2-3.

[viii] Cordes, Colleen and Edward Miller, eds. "Fool's gold: A Critical Look at Children and Computers." www.alianceforchildhood.net

[ix] Wells, N., and Evans, G. "Nearby Nature: A Buffer of Life Stress among Rural Children." *Environment and Behavior.* 35. 2003. 311-330.

[x] Hammond, Richard. "Why Kids Are Natural Born Scientists." *New Scientist.* January 5, 2009.

[xi] Roszak, Theodore. *The Making of an Elder Culture: Reflections on the Future of America's Most Audacious Generation.* New Society Publishers, Gabriola Island, 2009.

[xii] Roszak, Theodore. *The Making of a Counter Culture: Reflections on the Technocratic Society and Its Youthful Opposition.* University of California Press: Berkeley,

1969.

[xiii] Bolen, Jean Shinoda. *Crones Don't Whine: Concentrated Wisdom for Juicy Women.* Conari Press: San Francisco, 2003.

[xiv] Roszak, Theodore. *The Making of an Elder Culture: Reflections on the Future of America's Most Audacious Generation.* New Society Publishers, Gabriola Island, 2009. 38-39

[xv] Robbins, John. *Healthy at 100: Scientifically Proven Secrets of the World's Healthiest and Longest-Lived Peoples.* New York: Ballantine, 2007.

[xvi] Tamer, Mary. "On the Chopping Block, Again." *Ed., the Magazine of the Harvard Graduate School of Education.* June 8, 2009.

[xvii] Louv, Richard. *Last Child in the Woods: Saving Our Children from Nature-Deficit Disorder.* New York: Algonquin, 2008. 86-98.

[xviii] Lane, Chadwick. "The Chemistry of Information Addiction." *Scientific American,* October 13, 2009.

[xix] Lindstrom, Martin. "You Love Your iPhone. Literally." NY Times. September 30, 2011

[xx] De Waal, Franz. *The Age of Empathy: Nature's Lessons for Kinder Society.* Three Rivers Press, 2010.

[xxi] Salmon, Andrew. "Couple: Internet Gaming Addiction Led to Baby's Death." *CNN World.* April 1, 2010. http://articles.cnn.com/2010-04-01/world/korea.parents.starved.baby_1_gaming-addiction-internet-gaming-gaming-industry?_s=PM:WORLD

[xxii] Hall, C. Margaret. *The Special Mission of Grandparents: Hearing, Seeing, Telling.* Bergen and Garvey, Westport, 1999. 65.

[xxiii] Johnston, Lauren. *Rubber Duckies Map the World.* CBS Evening News with Katie Couric, cbsnews.com. May 19, 2010

224

[xxiv] Ramalho, Marina. "Amazon Rainforest Relies on African Dust." *SciDev Net.* January 10, 2007. http://www.scidev.net/en/news/amazon-rainforest-relies-on-african-dust.html

[xxv] Kornhaber, Arthur. *Contemporary Grandparenting.* Thousand Oaks: Sage Publishing, 1996.

[xxvi] Kornhaber, Arthur. *Contemporary Grandparenting.* Thousand Oaks: Sage Publishing, 1996.58

[xxvii] Maslow, A.H. "A Theory of Human Motivation." *Psychological Review.* 50.4. 1943.370-96.

[xxviii] Roszak, Theodore. *The Voice of the Earth: An Exploration of Ecopsychology.* New York: Simon and Shuster, 1992.

[xxix] Durning, Alan Thein. "Are We Happy Yet?" *Ecopsychology: Restoring the Earth, Healing the Mind.* Eds. Theodore Roszak, et al. San Francisco, Sierra Club, 1995.

[xxx] Wilson, Edward O. *Biophilia.* Harvard University Press, 1984.

[xxxi] Kingsolver, Barbara, et al. *Animal, Vegetable, Miracle: A Year of Food Life.* New York: Harper Collins, 2007

[xxxii] Elkind, David. *The Hurried Child: Growing Up Too Fast Too Soon.* Cambridge, De Capo, 2001.

[xxxiii] Coyle, Kevin J. "Back to School: Back Outside." World Wildlife Federation. September 2010.

[xxxiv] Barlow, Jim. "Children with ADHD Benefit from Time Outdoors Enjoying Nature." News Bureau Illinois. August 27, 2004.

[xxxv] Whitehouse, David. "Half of Humanity Set to Go Urban." *BBC News.* May 19, 2005.

[xxxvi] Lehrer, Johnas. "How the City Hurts Your Brain." *Boston Globe.* January 2, 2009.

[xxxvii] Kaplan, Rachel, and Stephen Kaplan. *The Experience of Nature: A Psychological Perspective.* Cambridge UP, 1989.

xxxviii Clements, R.. "An Investigation of the Status of Outdoor Play." *Contemporary Issues in Early Childhood*, 5.1. 68-80. 2004.

xxxix Francis, Mark (interview) with Kathryn Devereaux. "Children of Nature." *U. C. Davis Magazine.* 9.2 University of California, Davis. 1991.

xl Pyle, Robert. "Eden in a Vacant Lot: Special Places, Species and Kids in Community of Life." *Children and Nature: Psychological, Sociocultural and Evolutionary Investigations.* Eds. Kahn, P.H. and Kellert, S.R. Cambridge: MIT Press, 2002.

xli White, Randy. "Interaction with Nature During the Middle Years: Its Importance to Children's Development and Nature's Future." White Hutchinson Leisure and Learning Group, 2004
xlii Washuk, Bonnie. "All Auburn Kindergarten Students Getting iPads This Fall." *Sun Journal.* April 7, 2011
xliii Louv, Richard. *The Nature Principle.* New York: Algonquin, 2011.
xliv Gardner, Howard. "Revaluating Intelligence." BigThink.com http://bigthink.com/howardgardner#!video_idea_id=16279
xlv Pink, Daniel. *A Whole New Mind: Why Right Brainers Will Rule the Future.* New York: Riverhead Books, 2005.
xlvi Reistad-Long, Sara. "Older Brain May Really Be a Wiser Brain." *New York Times.* May 20, 2008.

xlvii *The Human Spark.* PBS. Episode 1. January 6, 2009.
xlviii Brown, Lester. "Ecopsychology and the

Environmental Revolution." *Ecopsychology.* xiii.

[xlix] Cohen, Michael. *Reconnecting with Nature: Finding Wellness through Restoring Your Bond with Nature.* Corvallis, OR: Ecopress, 1997.

[l] Silverstein, Merril, and Sarah Ruiz. "Breaking the Chain: How Grandparents Modest Create the Transmission of Maternal Depression to Their Grandchildren." *Family Relations* 55:5 (2006) 601- 612.

[li] Silverstein, Merril, and Sarah Ruiz. "Breaking the Chain: How Grandparents Modest Create the Transmission of Maternal Depression to Their Grandchildren." *Family Relations* 55:5 (2006) 601- 612.

[lii] Thompson, Andres. "How Many Species Exist on Earth." Science: msn.com. www.msnbc.msn.com/id/20109284/ns/technology_and_science-science/

[liii] United Nations. "International Migration, Racism, Discrimination, and Xenophobia." UN Commission for Human Rights, 2001. www.ilo.org/public/libdoc/ilo/2001/101B09_218_engl.pdf

[liv] Anonymous. "A Global Generation Gap: Adapting to a New World." The Pew Research Center for the People and the Press. February 24, 2004. http://people-press.org/commentary/?analysisid=86

[lv] Keltner, Dacher. Born to Be Good: The Science of a Meaningful Life. New York: Norton, 2009.

[lvi] "About Stromatolites." December 27, 2011. www.fossilmall.com/Science/About_Stromatolite.htm

[lvii] Heimbuch, Jaymi. "Nature Makes Us Nicer People, New Study Says." www.treehugger.com/files/2009/10/nature-makes-us-nicer-people-new-study-says.php

[lviii] Khamsi, Roxanne. "People Do Mellow with Age, Brain Scans Suggest." June 15, 2006. http://www.newscientist.com/article/dn9344-people-do-

mellow-with-age-brain-scans-suggest.html

[lix] from RichardLouv.com

Made in the USA
Lexington, KY
04 July 2013